FOR A NEW RUSSIA

Anatoly Sobchak

FOR A NEW RUSSIA

The Mayor of St. Petersburg's Own Story of the Struggle for Justice and Democracy

THE FREE PRESS
A Division of Macmillan, Inc.
NEW YORK

Maxwell Macmillan Canada
TORONTO

Maxwell Macmillan International
NEW YORK   OXFORD   SINGAPORE   SYDNEY

The Free Press
A Division of Macmillan, Inc.
866 Third Avenue, New York, N.Y. 10022

Maxwell Macmillan Canada, Inc.
1200 Eglinton Avenue East
Suite 200
Don Mills, Ontario M3C 3N1

Macmillan, Inc. is part of the Maxwell Communication
Group of Companies.

Printed in the United States of America

printing number
1   2   3   4   5   6   7   8   9   10

Library of Congress Cataloging-in-Publication Data

Sobchak, Anatoly,
    For a new Russia : the Mayor of St. Petersburg's own story of the
struggle for justice and democracy / Anatoly Sobchak.
        p.   cm.
    ISBN 0-02-929770-2
    1. Leningrad (R.S.F.S.R.)—History.   2. Sobchak, Anatoly.
3. Soviet Union—Politics and government—1985–   4. Perestroĭka.
5. Mayors—Soviet Union—Biography.   I. Title.
DK568.S64   1992
947'.45—dc20   91–35872
                                                        CIP

Photo credits: B. Babanov, A. Zemlyanichenko, A. Nikolayev, I. Nasov, Yu. Rost, L. Sherstennikov, and IAN (Novosti's international press service)

Cover photo: Novosti Information Agency

Contents

The Great Turn Towards Man

Valentin Berestov, a Moscow poet, wrote these lines about a boy before the war:

In those days
*   affairs of state*
Would feature
*   in my dreams.*
In two of these
*   before the war*
Kalinin came to me.

I never dreamt of affairs of state in my childhood. Once, at a very difficult time in my life, just after I had turned forty, I dreamt that I said everything I thought on the podium of the Kremlin Palace of Congresses about our political system and about the party's leaders, while Brezhnev and his chief of ideology, Suslov, listened with stone faces. Not being a member of the party, I woke up in a cold sweat.

Ten years later, when neither Brezhnev nor Suslov were around, my dream came true as I found myself on the same rostrum actually saying those same words that had stuck in my throat a decade earlier. It just so happens that now my office is located in the building of the Supreme Soviet opposite the Lenin Library, and its front is adorned by a memorial plaque announcing that the premises had once housed the reception room of Mikhail Kalinin, for a long time Chairman of the Presidium of the USSR Supreme Soviet.

People in civilized countries as a rule have little interest in politics. Will the average citizen spend days and nights in front of his TV set watching live reports of legislative debates if his country's government has functioned for several centuries and its political machinery runs with efficiency? Of course not—there are things which are much more interesting to this blessed citizen, such as business, culture, or sport.

It is a different story in countries with totalitarian regimes where one's life depends on political conditions but where, quite paradoxically, politics as such does not exist. The squabbling of flatterers around the throne and the games played by apparatchiks, perhaps—anything but politics.

Ours is a peculiar situation: the last of the world's empires, the Soviet Union, is falling apart, totalitarianism is bankrupt and national parliaments are being born. We are not at all sure that in a year or even six months from now our legislative bodies will exist as they do today. It may be that the republics, having acquired sovereignty, will find a different form of regulating their relations, and perhaps the Supreme Soviet will be transformed into a new state or international body. Be that as it may, history will note that the birth of a parliamentary system began in our country in the spring of 1989 in Moscow at the First Congress of People's Deputies of the USSR.

Imagine you are on an oceanliner and its barometer is forecasting a storm, and the new skipper orders his crew to increase speed in order to escape the danger zone and reach port before the storm begins. And then it turns out that the engines have come to the end of their servicing life, the propeller is damaged and the crew consists of hopeless landlubbers. During the ensuing panic someone hastens to procure a life jacket while another attempts to get hold of the only lifeboat on the grounds that it used to belong lawfully to his grandfather. And the ship's cook would rather drown than reach the shore because he will be tried there for embezzlement.

At this point the captain asks the passengers to form an alternative crew and repair the engine.

Thus we have, instead of a routine voyage, a soul-stirring drama. It is best to be watching it outside from the bridge or, at least, to be the captain's opponent, unaware of the gravity of the situation.

Neither I, nor my fellow deputies elected to the First Congress suspected that we had already become actors in a great social drama.

But the logic of events and the logic of conscience demanded that in a year some of the captain's consistent critics should start to steer the ship and modify its machinery without stopping the vessel. I was elected Chairman of the Leningrad City Council in the spring of 1990, and thus became responsible not only for the state of affairs of my country but also, and above all, for the destiny of my city. I certainly am well aware of the irony whereby I and my fellow democrats Boris Yeltsin and Gavril Popov often have had to depend on the very system that we have tried to transform. Government looks different from the inside, even at the municipal level, from what it looks like from the outside. I would like to describe without delay what it looks like to me, since the true course of events is being increasingly distorted by retrospective assessments.

Many people simply ignored Mikhail Gorbachev's words at the 27th Party Congress on the necessity for every person to be equal before the law regardless of his station in life. After all, Gorbachev's predecessors had said quite a few correct and just things in their reports to party congresses. It was only the professionals—political scientists and lawyers—who noted that the argument for equality before the law had been extended to party workers for the first time in seven decades. Never before in Soviet history had the subject of "law and the Party" been spoken about in an official speech by any party leader, nor had the legal position of the Communist Party been discussed in any scholarly paper or article.

The idea of separating state power from party power was Gorbachev's first blow at the all-embracing monopoly of the administrative system. Newspapers and academic journals began increasingly to print articles critical of "telephone rule," the sanctioned illegal actions of the party apparatchiks and the party's incompetent or selfish interference in the non-political sphere of public life. A little later, another, very important step would be taken at the 19th Party Conference, when Gorbachev would stress the necessity of dividing power. The question would at once arise as to what kind of state it would be in which power would be divided into legislative, executive and judiciary, and the party would be left only the sphere of ideology?

The answer was in the question itself, which formulated the idea of a law-governed society ruled not by arbitrariness, not by ideological precepts laid down in specific paragraphs of the Party Central Committee's political instructions and decisions, but by law. When we stopped to think for the first time what a law-governed society was, we suddenly discovered a very simple truth, known to the whole civilized world, that the idea of law is one of the universal human principles evolved over thousands of years. The affirmation of the primacy of law over the state compelled us to think in a new way of the very idea of law, and drop the notorious "class approach to law" which made possible the justification of any crime committed by the party, and any violence, expropriation or genocide according to the specifics of "class struggle" or the utopia of world proletarian revolution.

For seven decades we began every undertaking with a decision by the party and government, and each of them resulted in the shedding of the blood and tears of our people, and crimes being committed against mankind, our own people and our own land. It was not a matter of the evil personalities of some officials, or of Stalins, Berias, or Radishovs, but of the intrinsically inhuman essence of the system of power built on the blood of the people by the party of the "triumphant proletariat."

What we attest to today is that any undertaking should begin and end not with a resolution but with man. Law is only a necessary means of maintaining order in society, an instrument not of the state's manipulation of man, as of a cog in the state machine, but a means of appealing to man, and to his earthly needs and grievances. A law-governed society begins with the recognition of these simple truths. Of course, the establishment of whatever replaces the Soviet system, in which man is not a little cog and not even an abstract "human factor" but an intransient eternal asset, will require the labor of many generations.

The declaration of the priority of universal human values over all others, including class ones, forced me to give up what was a tranquil, quite satisfactory and even prosperous life as a Leningrad professor of civil and economic law. I took what was said from the rostrum of the 19th Party Conference as an appeal to everyone, including myself, for civic mobilization. When words began to be supported by deeds and Gorbachev announced the withdrawal of Soviet troops from Afghanistan, I, who was not a party member, applied for membership in the Communist Party.

When I decided to take this step, which was not popular even then, I made no secret with anyone, least of all myself, of the fact that the CPSU was to me above all not a political party but a state structure permeating every cell of the country's social organism. This knowledge led me to believe that reforms in our society could begin only through party reform and the engendering of democratic politics.

As a people's deputy of the Leningrad City Council and of the USSR, I certainly have no idea, now in mid-December 1990, since completing the dictation of this book to Andrei Chernov, an observer from the *Moscow News*, who has agreed to write it down, what tomorrow has in store for us. But no matter what may await us after the fall of the sclerotic Soviet empire, these notes, if they are destined to see the light, will be for the future reader testimony of a witness of the great turn towards Man which is taking place and will occur, in spite of everything, in our society.

I lay no claim either to an exhaustive political assessment of events or to exceptional objectivity in my narration. This is a story not of a historian or an impartial observer, but of a participant in events who was destined to be present during the birth of a legislature and became one of the actors in the drama of parliamentary democracy.

Chronology

1988

June 28:   At the 19th Party Conference, General Secretary Mikhail Gorbachev proposes a major reorganization of the Soviet government, including a new elective legislature to be called the Congress of People's Deputies.

1989

January 10:   Campaigning begins across the USSR for seats in the new Congress of People's Deputies.

February 15:   The last Soviet troops withdraw from Afghanistan.

March 26:   Nationwide elections for the Congress of People's Deputies begin.

April 8–9:   Nineteen citizens are killed in Tbilisi, Georgia, when riot police and soldiers attack a peaceful demonstration. A commission of People's Deputies, chaired by Anatoly Sobchak, would later investigate major Party bosses concerning their role in the decision to send troops into Tbilisi.

April 10:   Anatoly Sobchak wins a seat in the Vasilievsky Ostrov district of Leningrad as a delegate to the new Congress of People's Deputies.

May 18:   Lithuania, Estonia, and Latvia introduce bills declaring their sovereignty.

May 22–25:   The First Congress of People's Deputies opens in Moscow to a live nationwide TV audience, and the members of the permanent legislature, the Supreme Soviet, are elected. In June, the Inter-Regional Group, comprised of over two hundred People's Deputies and led by Boris Yeltsin, Andrei Sakharov and other liberals, is organized to coordinate parliamentary activity and strategy.

June 3:   The Supreme Soviet opens its first session. Led by People's Deputies, it rejects many new ministerial appointments to posts in the new government, and forces many resignations. Soviet premier Nikolai Ryzkov is investigated for endorsing an apparat-run enterprise, ANT, revealed to be selling tanks illegally.

September 25: The Supreme Soviet begins its second session.

November 9: Two weeks after the Warsaw Pact nations endorse the right of each to choose its own political direction, the Berlin Wall is destroyed, symbolizing the end of Soviet domination and communist ideology in Central and Eastern Europe.

November 22: Boris Gidaspov, the Leningrad regional party chief, attempts a putsch, taking over as city party boss and launching a well-coordinated media campaign and rally designed to recall many local democratic deputies. The putsch fails.

December 12: The Second Congress of People's Deputies opens. Two days later, December 14, Andrei Sakharov, physicist, Nobel Peace Prize winner, and a People's Deputy, dies.

1990

February 4: Following their counterparts in Eastern Europe, one-half million people protest in Moscow on the eve of the plenary session of the Communist Party Central Committee, whose members will vote almost unanimously to repeal Article 6 of the Soviet constitution, which guarantees the party's monopoly on ideology and politics.

March 13: The Third Congress of People's Deputies repeals Article 6 and elects Gorbachev president.

May 1: Gorbachev is jeered in Red Square at the annual May Day parade.

June 1: Anatoly Sobchak is elected chairman of the Leningrad City Council and later elected mayor of Leningrad.

June 19: The Russian Communist Party Congress opens in Moscow.

June 22: Ivan Polozkov is elected leader of the Russian Communist Party.

July 2: The 28th Communist Party Congress opens. Yegor Ligachev loses his bid for deputy party chief after interrogation about complicity in the decision to send troops to Tbilisi.

July 13: Sobchak and other reformist Deputies resign from the Communist Party.

October 15: Mikhail Gorbachev is awarded the 1990 Nobel Peace Prize.

October 16: Gorbachev adopts weakened economic reform package after rejecting Stanislav Shatalin's more sweeping 500-day plan.

December 20: Foreign Minister Eduard Shevardnadze resigns, warning of an impending dictatorship.

1991

January 7–13: Soviet Army troops attack and occupy the Lithuanian capital of Vilnius.

August 19–20: Right-wing and nationalist forces arrest Gorbachev and attempt a Kremlin coup.

August 20–21: Boris Yeltsin in Moscow and Anatoly Sobchak in Leningrad enlist public support to put down the coup.

September 6: The Supreme Soviet of the Russian Republic decrees that Leningrad immediately resume its original name, St. Petersburg, in memory of Czar Peter I, who founded the city in 1703 and named it for his patron saint.

FOR A NEW RUSSIA

1

The Political Amateurs Arrive

We were lucky to be born in Russia
In these momentous years.

From a song

I was elected to the USSR Supreme Soviet in June 1989. This new standing Soviet Parliament was to go into session two weeks after the First Congress of People's Deputies, to which I, and several hundred other new deputies, had been elected that spring. Given the opportunity, I decided to stay in Moscow to get the feel of the city and take a look around.

Each Supreme Soviet member was given a room in the Moskva Hotel, not far from the Kremlin Wall and the Eternal Flame, which burns in memory of the Unknown Soldier. The hotel, as gargantuan in scale as Stalin's state power, offers its guests few comforts. It has been there for fifty years and Muscovites are used to it, but a visitor can't help noticing the bizarre asymmetry of its facade. An invisible vertical line seems to divide it in two, with one architectural style on the left, another on the right. As the story goes, the architect worked up two designs, and Stalin, not realizing that they were different, signed off on both. Nobody had the temerity to explain this mistake to the "Father of Peoples." So the hotel was built using both designs.

Each of us had a tiny single room. As the months went by, our

1

rooms became increasingly cluttered with papers—letters, appeals, draft laws, and telegrams from all over the country. On my windowsill and under my bed, in the closet and on top of the TV, papers everywhere. The table was a mess and the mountain threatened to come down in an avalanche, especially if I opened the door and the window at the same time.

We were parliamentary pioneers, lacking aides, technical support, money—and, more critically—lacking experience. Nor had Moscow ever before coped with as many as 500 deputies swarming in from all over the nation. None of us had the faintest idea how to organize the workday, let alone the evening. Considering the diversity of our ages, backgrounds, and interests, we must have looked like overage inhabitants of a student dormitory.

Russians from the provinces describe Moscow by saying "It's an exciting place, but I could never live there. Everyone's always in such a hurry." Life in the capital does move at a faster pace, in the streets, the subway, offices, even the stores. But size is not the only determining feature. Moscow is the "brain" of a huge body, and it has to move faster than the rest of the country. It pulses with a rhythm that, to the average provincial Russian, verges on the inhuman. The pace of this life slows as it spreads in concentric circles from the center, subsiding a it reaches the suburbs. Russian writers felt the same rapid imperial heartbeat back when St. Petersburg was Russia's capital. Gogol, a provincial by birth, marveled at the city's "forty thousand couriers alone." Moscow, then only "a big village," was a lethargic kingdom of past glories. But that Moscow is long gone.

The thing that most amazed me, after my election, was that just a few months earlier I couldn't have imagined a life beyond the book shelves, library walls, or comfort of my study. My wife and I lived with our younger daughter in a modest three-room apartment in Leningrad. My study doubled as a child's room, and my young daughter Ksenia liked to explain to guests that she "leased" a corner to her father. In those days, after the kids' goodnight TV program, I would take my papers to the living room to prepare for the next day's work. By Soviet standards, these were more than adequate accommodations for a university professor, considering that about half of all Leningrad families still live in communal apartments.

After my election, every morning, rain or shine, I would walk from the Moskva to work in the Kremlin, and it still seemed unreal to me. A letter addressed merely to "Sobchak, Leningrad University," might conceivably have reached me in the past if someone had bothered to send one, but since joining Congress, thousands of letters I have received have been marked simply "Sobchak, Kremlin, Moscow." The letters and visitors coming in from places whose names I had never before heard seemed proof of television's remarkable new influence on our society. Without the mass media, without Mikhail Gorbachev prevailing on the Politburo to allow live broadcasts from the Congress, the initial phase of democratization would have taken years longer, despite the fact that the pot was ready to boil over. And the nation was watching us. For a while, we deputies stole the limelight from TV stars, soccer players, singers, fashion designers. Television provided an outlet for political expression and gave us a bit more hope that many of our country's historical deadlocks and injustices would be resolved.

Before then the public had held only vague impressions of the men and women who represented them. But after the newly televised Congress began, average citizens were in effect "re-electing" their deputies—not by ballot, but by debate. In just a few days, some deputies, having become household names, lost constituents' confidence and interest, while others earned voters' trust. Every Soviet family was talking *deputies*. But by late June it was clear that the TV coverage of the parliamentary debates was too costly—not the airtime, but production downtime—because of the fact that everyone, workers included, was riveted to the television screen.

Working in parliament was like living in a television. You mixed with the famous—people you used to see only on TV or read about in the paper. You ran the risk that your old friends would become disgruntled and jealous. Some would suspect you of putting on airs and take offense when you declined their invitations to birthday parties. You couldn't blame them; even my wife and daughter at times rolled their eyes enviously at my tales of legislative adventure.

Like a typical Leningrader, I have never been all that fond of Moscow. As a city, it lacks shape and symmetry. But, as I said, it does have the rapid tempo that comes from being at the center of the action. To a provincial, every Muscovite carries a bit of the aura of nobility. Muscovites, aware of this, tend to flaunt their intimacy with power. Since there are more job and career opportunities in Moscow than anywhere else, it attracts very talented and ambitious people. Acquaintanceships are easy to strike up. Personalities stand out.

At the Lenkom theatre during those first days of Parliament, I got to know the poet Yevgeny Yevtushenko. It was the first time we had met and we talked into the wee hours. We were both children of

the thaw of the early 60s, "blood brothers." We had read the same
books and seen the same movies. We shared a history. Who would
ever have imagined the rebel Yevtushenko, years after he had thrilled
us with his early lyrics, writing a twenty-five word poem to be adopted
as the oath sworn by the first Soviet president—and no one blinking
an eye.

Also at the opening were the film director Eldar Ryazanov, and
the actor Yevgeni Leonov, who, offstage, is charming and witty.

At a premiere at the Malaya Bronnaya Theater, I met yet another luminary, the writer Venedikt Yerofeyev. His novel *Moscow-
Petushki** published in samizdat had been deeply influential
throughout the country. He lived to see his book published officially
and an adaptation staged, but he was already a very sick man. Unfortunately, our first meeting proved to be our last. It seems the wave
of deaths in the early 80s, people dying before the end of the "old
days," was being followed by another wave of deaths of people who
had lived just long enough to see the new age in.

But our time was hardly up. We were just beginning this arduous and often thankless business of carrying out perestroika, of which
we ourselves were a part. None of us was a Hercules, but it was our
job to clean the Augean stables of totalitarianism. The public who
talked about "popovs" and "sobchaks" lusting for power couldn't
really have meant us. After all, we were only political amateurs learning our parts in the democratic drama that was unfolding.

* *Moscow Circles*—a down and out in Moscow style novel—*ed.*

2

Elections According to Gorbachev

And all those government buildings
Blood-blistered by snow and rain.
Blind-eye cataracts at their windows—
(For ages alone and friendless)
Faceless faces of leaders of men.

       —Alexander Galich, "An Attempt at Nostalgia"*

The Call

Backroom politics and pre-election machinations were in full swing and the city of Leningrad teemed with meetings and gatherings. Candidates for Parliament were determined to get their names on the ballot, even if they had to nominate themselves. I was just a spectator, with nothing to do with the campaigning. I was immersed in my professional work—lectures, academic committee meetings, article-writing. I had cast a skeptical eye on the cumbersome and not very democratic system Gorbachev had concocted to conduct the first Soviet parliamentary elections. Little did I suspect that soon, I too would be sucked into this electoral whirlpool.

But then, at a meeting of my own department, the law department at the University of Leningrad, my name came up, proposed unexpectedly by an assistant professor and former pupil of mine.

* From *Alexander Galich: Songs & Poems*, translated and edited by Gerald Stanton Smith (Ann Arbor, MI: Ardis, 1983), p. 180.

The meeting had begun with the chairman, the head of our trade union bureau, telling us that we'd been given the chance to nominate our own candidates but cautioning that candidacies had already been proposed by some major industrial enterprises, in particular the Baltiysky shipbuilding plant. We knew that those were the likeliest nominees, especially since our district, Vasilievsky Ostrov, an industrial section of Leningrad, had been represented in the Supreme Soviet for the past fifty years by senior workers of the plant. Of course, we had the option of nominating our own people, said the meeting chairman, but it would be advisable for us to support the Baltiysky plant's nominee. It would, he said, be preferable from every practical point of view. We would save time; we could put the nomination to a vote and end the meeting. Those in favor . . ., etc.

But the chairman's view was not endorsed. We nominated six people, all of them well-known and respected members of our department, including myself.

Of course, I had no time to prepare a platform, but, as soon as I opened my mouth during this meeting, I realized that key questions about life in our long-suffering society, the hot spots and blind alleys and possible ways of averting impending crises, had been on my mind for ages.

Words about the need for a law-governed state, the priority of common human values over class interests, the necessity of a new approach for ensuring human rights, rolled off my tongue. I spoke enthusiastically about reforming the economy, of new ideas for industrial accountability, and of the independence for the republics.

At the caucus of the university's work collective, shortly thereafter, eleven nominees convened on stage. But ever after I won nearly three-quarters of the votes and was the only candidate to make it to the electoral ward meeting, I still could not quite believe this electoral business in which I had become a participant.

The Bet

As the popular saying goes, "You don't bet against the state." This includes state-run lotteries and alleged "elections." So, I considered the first intra-university stages of the electoral process as insider games, taking advantage of the chance to show off a bit. Then, I ran into one of the city's party hacks, an old acquaintance, in a university corridor. "Listen," he said, "You don't want to get involved in politics. You're a smart guy, you know there's no chance you'll be elected. The deputy will be a working-class hero from the Baltiysky plant. Don't waste your time." But like a kid, all of a sudden I felt the urge to be "king of the mountain." So I challenged him.

We made a gentleman's bet on the spot. The stakes? A bottle of brandy. To give this guy his due, he anted up the bottle two months later without prompting. The bottle of brandy, a truly precious commodity in perestroika-era Leningrad, eventually accompanied me to Moscow where my fellow deputies would come to my hotel room after sessions for all kinds of legal advice, bringing along bottles of their own, in the usual Russian style. (This practice was one of the reasons why I, not much of a drinker, found it necessary to move eventually from the hotel to an apartment.)

That Leningrad apparatchik must have really stung my ego. But he wasn't the first to cast a skeptical eye on my behavior. What really riled me was hearing friends and colleagues say, "Do you really believe all this election nonsense? Genuine elections aren't possible in this country. Don't you understand why ward meetings have been introduced? Can't you see you're sure to be voted down?"

Listening to them, I realized I could talk all I wanted without making a dent. The only way to prove anything was to win. But the contest was still a long way off. For now, I could only shrug agreement that, to a lawyer, this election stuff was only of professional interest. But by then I was committed to the battle. The times were changing. The era of stagnation was over. It was possible to snatch victory even in the face of an unsystematic and undemocratic electoral system.

As a political novice, I could only act on my intuition, something lawyers need no less than poets.

The news from the election committee specified that each body that had nominated or thrown its support behind a candidate was to send three representatives to the local ward meeting. So, I said to myself, I could count on three votes. But how could I lure away supporters from my rivals? I could ask for backing from other organizations—each one would mean three more votes. But I knew that my principal opponents already had support from as many as seventy such organizations apiece. The numbers were stacked against me—the worker from the Baltiysky plant by then had 207 supporters in the hall, against my hearty three. It didn't take much to see that an attempt to scrape up enough votes to win would be futile. And I still had my university obligations—lectures, teaching, departmental administration.

Half of the participants in this newfangled ward meeting represented organizations which had nominated or supported a candidate. The other half, however, represented the general public or work collectives. Their choice of candidate was a matter between themselves and their conscience. And so I decided to aim my pitch at them.

The way the election was organized, a candidate from, say, a kindergarten with ten employees, and one from the more than thirty-thousand-strong collective at the university, each got three votes. But this "equal opportunity" approach did leave one tiny opening for a desperado aware that he had to rely on his wits. A lone fighter needs brains, agility, and first rate preparation. That's why I carefully calculated a strategy, rather than running around academic departments trying to scrounge a few votes here and a few there.

The Ward Meeting

Not unexpectedly, at the Baltiysky plant's palace of culture, where workers met to conduct social activities, their nominee's visage was plastered all over the walls and featured at stands displaying special newspaper issues, stickers, and the like. The other, less powerful nominees had one puny stand apiece. Mine featured an article from the Leningrad University newspaper and a student-written leaflet extolling my alleged political virtues.

That night a crowd milled around the entrance, while admission passes were checked scrupulously, to the indignation of electors not permitted in the hall. Bouncers with red armbands stood ready to suppress excessive manifestations of civic initiative. A similar filtering process had been much in evidence at ward meetings in Leningrad, and countrywide, throughout this election campaign.

Each of the eleven nominees had ten minutes to speak, another ten minutes in which to answer questions. We'd drawn lots to determine the order of appearance. I drew number ten, affording me hours to watch my rivals in action. Some flopped right away, and clearly didn't stand a chance. Others seemed quite convincing, and I could see I had a real battle before me. It was exciting to watch how some nominees scored points and others lost them, and to track the audience's reactions.

When a well-known metalworker from the plant stood up to speak, his chances clearly looked good—especially since his plant bused in participants to the meeting. They'd provided the transport; all you had to provide was your vote. They set up refreshments in a lobby, excellent stuff by current standards, while Leningrad newspapers had written up their candidate on several occasions. On top of all this, he was chairman of the council of the production association's many-thousand-strong work collective. He was the hero of the day.

But the hero fell flat on his face when someone asked him to comment on the Brezhnev years. The "worker," his hands looking suspiciously soft, blurted out:

"They were the most wonderful years of my life! I worked well! My life was full!"

No youngster, he suddenly radiated youthful ardor. It was understandable; those were the years when he began to sit in high-level meetings, collect decorations, ride in a chauffeured car. That's when he arrived—and, as the saying goes, "began to pitch for Soviet power."

The Baltiysky worker had no trouble outscoring this rival. His speech was clumsy but direct. "I am for the workers, I'll defend their interests. I believe workers' interests should be protected by workers, since all those professors don't know how workers live." This strong, imposing man captured the audience with his sweeping gestures, his sincerity and his abject artlessness.

"I, Too, Have a Dream"

It was 11:30 P.M. by the time my turn came. Although I'm an improviser by nature, I prepared my speech in detail. I'd planned to talk about the special virtues of a law-governed state and a market economy. But as my hand crept to my jacket pocket for my notes I realized if I stuck to my prepared text I'd blow it. The audience had been sitting for more than six hours, and the last thing they needed was a lecture. Feverishly, I tried to come up with something. My mind went blank. The microphone staring me in the face and the audience, blandly attentive, seemed to be saying to me: "Come on, professor, spit it out."

And then Martin Luther King's "I Have a Dream" speech popped into my mind. I summoned up the ghost of the great American civil rights crusader, and declared that I too had a dream: of a time when there would be no ward meetings or preliminary selection of nominees, when electors would be able to nominate a candidate without having their closed-door meetings "protected" by squads of public security volunteers and militia; when greedy, incompetent leaders would lose the power to reduce our lives to absurdity; when the minister of land improvement and water resources who buried billions of rubles in the ground, the finance minister who'd concealed an immense budget deficit, and the chairman of the Supreme Court, who'd made his career by denouncing his colleagues, would find themselves out of a job. I dreamed of a time when our state would become law-governed—a state that didn't permit the granting of rights and privileges to some people at the expense of others.

I didn't "dream" for long in front of that exhausted crowd. But when I finished, and there was a hush, I knew I'd won them over.

When the votes were counted I was the number 2 votegetter. The Baltiysky worker was number 3. Number 4 was a stoker from another part of the town. And number 1, by an impressive one hundred votes, was a foreman from the Kronstadt naval yard, a talented man. The four of us were duly registered by the ward meeting as nominees for the First People's Congress. It was, as things turned out, the most democratic ward in Leningrad.

The meeting ended around 2 A.M. City buses don't run this late, so on that February night, our group walked across town, discussing excitedly the ins and outs of the electoral battle ahead. Somewhere near the Petrograd subway station we managed to flag down a private cab whose driver was a former student of mine who recognized me. As he listened to us talking, he told me he worked in a boring office by day and drove around by night to supplement his wages. Not surprisingly, he earned ten times more in a night than in an eight-hour day at the office.

"Aren't you afraid of picking up passengers so late?" I asked.

"No, I can take care of myself. But tell me, Anatoly Alexandrovich, what do you want with all this election business? It's all lies and games, Gorbachev and his elections. No matter what you do, you won't be able to overthrow the system. I can understand if you're tired of your professional life and feel like playing games, but I pity you if you're serious. The system's a brick wall. It can't be pulled down by professors."

I admit that this conversation put a damper on my euphoria. Yes, you could win, I told myself, but *then* what?

But now I had to banish such thoughts, because the election campaign was gearing up. Soon, I would find myself speaking at a hundred and more meetings and rallies. I would win my first electoral fight thanks to two innovations I introduced into the city's public life. First, I began addressing the public through a bullhorn near the two subway stations in my ward. One is at the center of Vasilievsky Ostrov, the other in the Golodai area, on the gulf beach. Tens of thousands of people pass these places every morning and evening. They wait for overcrowded buses and trams, read newspapers, smoke, or simply stare at the low northern sky.

Vasileostrovskaya, a glass dome that stands above a small square, is, as I discovered, particularly well suited for election campaigning. All I had to do was stand near the entrance and go to work on my idle electors.

The Vasileostrovskaya station became a permanent campaign spot and, eventually, a political "outpost," a kind of Leningrad Hyde Park. Candidates running for the Supreme Soviet of the Russian Federation now use it as a canvassing center. And month after month, the city's "informals," from the left-wing Popular Front to the right-wing Pamyat, would crowd around portable stands there to make their pitch to whomever would listen.

During the 1989 elections, people eventually would gather there every day, whether or not I showed up.

The second innovation was Western-style television debates. I'd been doing the "Law and Economic Life" program on Leningrad television for a while, so I managed to convince the TV authorities that Leningrad needed these televised political debates. This was a first for our county.

I drew my preparation for the debates from my experience at the subway stations listening to people who, although they were half-awake or tired after a day's work, still got engaged in heated arguments about things that they were indifferent to just yesterday.

As a result of my electioneering, I learned a lot about where I stood on the issues. In part, this was because it was exceedingly clear who was leading the campaign against me: overzealous rivals and sullen district-level party functionaries.

Scenes from a Campaign

One morning a middle-aged woman yelled from the subway steps: "Elect this egghead? No way. A bunch of good-for-nothings they are, especially Sobchak. The girls in his classes can forget about good grades unless they put out for him—yes, my niece was trying to get into the law department and Sobchak told her she could take the entrance exams—if she'd allow him to *take her* first. But she's a good girl, so no university for her."

The people around the woman nodded eagerly. "Yes, they're all the same!" Suddenly, a simply-dressed man burst out indignantly: "You idiots, listening to that stupid dame! Even if she's only half right, and if he's got the energy for a handful of those girls, he's got to be our man; he'll have enough energy to solve all our problems!"

A scene reported by my wife, a history lecturer at the Institute of Culture—who developed a certain taste for these meetings—went like this: Another sob-sister cried out to the crowd, "How can you listen to Sobchak? That brute—his wife's lying there in the hospital dying, and he doesn't bring her so much as an apple! The poor dear's in the same ward as my daughter."

Lyudmila, losing her cool, pulled out her passport and brandished it: "You see that? I'm Sobchak's wife. Where do you come off with this nonsense? Let's go down to the militia station and find out who *you* are and what you're up to . . ."

The lady took off like a rocket amid loud laughter.

And then there were the leaflets that so helpfully informed me that I was a shareholder in some cooperative that was helping the "shadow economy" rob the working people.

Yet another subject embraced by my opponents was my alleged intention to sterilize the working class. This began when a university law department colleague wrote in a book that alcoholics and drug addicts who cannot have normal children should be persuaded to agree to sterilization, rather than give birth to sick children. At a rally, asked how I felt about this, I answered that if a person agreed *voluntarily*, I saw nothing criminal in the idea.

My opponents promptly capitalized on this.

After a meeting at the Arctic and Antarctic Museum, someone standing beside my poster shouted that I wanted to castrate workers; "They have taken away their vodka," said the man. "Now, they are going to take away their women!"

The change in the crowd's mood was palpable. A muscular hand tore my photograph from the poster.

"What are you doing, that's not what he's for!" another young man interrupted. "He's all for you sleeping with your woman as much as you like, but without forcing her to have abortions if you're a drunkard and already have five mentally retarded kids!"

To my surprise, the first guy smoothed out my photo, muttering at it: "Sorry, pal, I didn't know."

This two month campaign gave me an entirely new perspective on life.

People generally spend their lives in their own milieu, which in the case of professors is a very understated one. They talk only to members of their own social circle, and their ideas about life inevitably become increasingly circumscribed. This is all the more true when you're in a comparatively well-off and comfortable stratum in which you call on your neighbors only to find out whether the lights are out on every floor or it's only your own fuse that's burned out.

The notions I'd gleaned from court cases or in revealing articles in *Literary Gazette* or *Ogonyok* weren't nearly so ugly and dreadful as the reality of people's lives. Nor had I any inkling of how fed up people were with absolutely *everything*—their homes, their jobs, their leaders, the state of our hospitals, their stores with their empty shelves, all the lies. . . . Never had I seen such a sea of suffering faces as I did during those two pre-election months. The conviction of the liberal Soviet intelligentsia that it "knows the people" simply recapitulates the misconceptions of the powers-that-be and party functionaries (who are even more cocooned from ordinary folk by their cordons of sycophants and their well-honed indolence and arrogance).

Never had I answered so many questions. How many? Thousands. Tens of thousands. The man in the street fires them off the cuff. It's not particularly important how profound or serious the question is. The trick is to take a hard look at yourself before you reply. Your answer thus becomes an act of self-cognition, a step forward, however small.

Most Frequently Asked Questions

During my two-month long baptism I was often asked about the role of the Communist Party and Article 6 of the USSR Constitution. It was not a hard one for me to answer; I'd always stood for party

pluralism and believed that the country's basic laws should not insti-
tutionalize the "leading role" of the Communist Party as Article 6 had
provided for. But I was always careful to say that party pluralism
couldn't be introduced by decree. The process of establishing political parties would be, necessarily, long and difficult.

Sometimes a question, seemingly frivolous or inane, still wasn't
easy to answer, like this well-aimed potshot:

"Why don't capitalists have Heroes of Capitalist Labor when we
have so many Heroes of Socialist Labor?"

You don't have a second to think about your answer at a public
meeting. I would snap right back that "over there" they work in order
to live, while we live in order to work, and that's why *our* work is
heroic. I seemed to have hit the mark—I got a laugh and the ques-
tioner nodded, satisfied.

"Why do our male leaders take their wives along on foreign trips
while Comrade Biryukova, a Central Committee member, doesn't
take along her husband?"

"That's a question for Comrade Biryukova to answer," I would
say; "she probably has her reasons. . . ."

This barely makes the grade, but the audience generously for-
gave a swift return if the ball rolled out of play.

Questions could be funny or vicious, could come from friends or
foes.

"Are you a Jew?"

"Oh, no, not a Jew, a Yid-Mason."

My utter exhaustion at the end of each day of campaigning was
no joke. I was barely able to say a word to my wife and daughter in
the evening. I had fantasies of blowing off this whole election business. Only pride, a far from commendable quality, kept me in the
race. What about the people who had come to put their faith in me?

A Team from Nowhere

The most unexpected result of the pre-election marathon was the
appearance on the scene of complete strangers to whom I became
unexpectedly close.

I started out on my own, without funds or backing. True, journalists from the university newspaper promptly offered their aid. The
university allocated 500 rubles to print campaign leaflets. These leaflets didn't come out until just before the election, but this turned out

to be a lucky stroke. As I mentioned earlier, Vasilievsky Ostrov had been plastered with my rivals' leaflets, and at every rally I was asked where my photographs and program were. I remained a dark horse until two days before the election, when my team finally received the packets of leaflets. The next day, my photo gazed back at me at every turn.

No one wins an election singlehandedly. Campaigns are collective undertakings. They hinge upon teamwork, and I had no team. University professors and their assistants may be amiable and bright and honorable folks, but it's hard to get them to do rounds of the streets at night with a can of glue and shopping bags full of leaflets, or to put aside scholarly work for electioneering, traipsing around with a metal bullhorn in all sorts of weather. Not even for a pal.

My makeshift team invented itself. That is, people—strangers to me and to each other—came up and said: "We want to help." They created my team and built my support, and, eventually, my victory. A few were students, but most had nothing to do with the university— engineers, cultural workers, manual laborers, including some from the Baltiysky plant. By the end I was no longer a lone toiler. There were fifty hardworking volunteers by my side.

Not surprisingly television debates were the decisive factor. The first round of voting was over before the TV authorities finally consented to the debates. Meanwhile, the electoral battle had heated up. I came within a one and a half per cent of victory in the first round. My opponent, the Kronstadt foreman, wasn't one to shirk a fight, and we were on screen for a good three and a half hours.

Election Day

After a rare good night's sleep I got up and cast my vote (for the candidate who eventually won in the north Leningrad district where I've lived for ages). Then my wife and I got out of town and forgot the damned election for a whole day. Results were due in the following day.

We were awakened at 2 A.M. by the telephone and were informed that I had won. Seventy-six percent—three-quarters of those who went to the polls—voted for me.

That date was April 10. Later that morning, I learned about the bloody confrontation in Tbilisi. I muttered to myself, told my wife the morons in generals' costumes were back to their old tricks—*use force, and hang the consequences.* We heard that there were victims; later, we learned that sixteen women were killed. The grim price of our wholesale amateurism was a knife in my heart. The official announcement was that the victims were "crushed" by the crowd. I thought of the people "crushed to death" on Khodynka Field before the 1917 revolution, and in 1953, during Stalin's funeral. (We'd not yet heard about the use of poison gas and engineers' shovels to disperse the crowd.)

I pushed Tbilisi out of my mind, where it would stay until the first Congress of People's Deputies. Over the decades we'd developed an immunity to bad news, a special Soviet enzyme in our blood that suppresses pain and anesthetizes our soul and conscience.

Other activities engaged my attention. For one thing, several of the newly elected Leningrad deputies were trying to put together at least the seeds of a parliamentary bloc. Soon after the election, we were invited to the regional party headquarters, where the first secretary, Yuri Solovyov, wasted no time "getting some sense into [our] heads." He laid out the scenario of the upcoming congress. But we cut him off rather brusquely and informed him that the deputies would be writing *this* scenario. He had no choice but to grin and bear it. But when I proposed that the deputies stick around to talk about assembling a Leningrad parliamentary bloc, he got nervous.

"No, not here! Do whatever you like, but not in Smolny" [the headquarters of the Leningrad Communist Party organization].

The next day, we convened at the Union of Journalists, which became our pre-congress headquarters. Moscow representatives soon showed up, and we got down to real work.

The Election "System"

Only much later did I realize why Gorbachev manufactured such a complex and utterly undemocratic, but ingenious, electoral system. The apparat, firmly and reliably entrenched after generations of party selection, wouldn't allow democrats a single chance to win direct and justly weighted elections carried out by secret ballot. A well-oiled system of bureaucratic procrastination, mutual backscratching, controlled mass media, money from party and state budgets, the power to pluck from regular jobs just about anyone needed for the campaign, paid support groups—these guaranteed success. But Gorbachev and his brain trust tossed the apparat into alien conditions where the Soviet tradition didn't work. Elections within public organizations and the USSR Academy of Sciences and the division of the country into territorial and national-territorial electoral wards opened up many new possibilities.* Such nationally celebrated names as Andrei Sakharov's were inscribed in the Parliament only thanks to Gorbachev's crafty "undemocratic" electoral system. The apparat used up its energies organizing ward meetings which became notorious for attempting to keep democrats from getting through their "filter." But public organizations didn't hold these ward meetings. And there were runoffs in some places. So, for example, when Vitaly Korotich, editor-in-chief of the magazine *Ogonyok*, walked out of a Moscow ward meeting to protest obvious rigging by the chairman, he was promptly nominated in the Ukrainian city of Kharkov, where he won by a large margin.

The "Voters' Advocate"

There was a minor tragedy in Leningrad, where the apparat had assigned electors to make certain that the head of the city party committee ran unopposed. As the meeting began, an excited, middle-aged man climbed the rostrum and demanded that both candidates' names be on the ballot. His voice faltered, he choked on his words; suddenly, he collapsed. The chairman told the meeting that the over-excited speaker had fainted. Doctors came and helped him. At the end of the meeting, they learned that the man had died. His last words were, "This may be our last chance." No one could forget these words . . . the handpicked electors were too shaken to knock the name of the "unwanted" candidate off the ballot, and he won easily.

The vagueness and ambiguity of the election law led to utter confusion. In many places, the apparat hadn't a clue how to conduct ward meetings. Secretaries of district party committees and chairmen of ward electoral commissions consulted me as a lawyer, so I was advising others as well as conducting my own campaign. The apparat's bewilderment was evident to me.

Glasnost did not yet mean freedom of speech. It is only a synonym of the Russian word *"oglaska"* (the opportunity to reveal the truth, to make facts public). Freedom of speech begins with, but is

---

*The complex election procedures include selection of candidates by group affiliation as well as by geographic district—*ed.*

not realized by, glasnost. Freedom of speech presupposes not only
the abolition of censorship but also the right of everyone to establish
a mass media, party plurality, and much more. It is true that glasnost
yielded fruit from the very start, as people began for the first time to
reveal in public what was in their hearts. What began to be said on
live radio and TV programs and on the stage never could have been
passed by even the boldest editors in the past. Even *Ogonyok*, one of
the boldest current magazines, sometimes seemed quite conservative
against this background.

The country had never before spoken so frankly and sharply.
Criticism of authorities and previously unthinkable attacks on the
party eroded the limits of "socialist pluralism." The hardest thing for
me to explain at meetings and rallies was why I recently joined the
party and was backing Gorbachev's perestroika. I said that here,
where the party had supplanted the state, an attempt to create a new
political system without democratizing the party was doomed, and
might precipitate a bloody civil war.

My constituents must have found my explanations satisfactory;
otherwise, I would not have received my mandate.

Thus, I embarked on a path that I had not chosen, and shouldered a burden for which I was not prepared.

During the election campaign a Leningrad journalist nicknamed
me "the voters' advocate." (It was flattering, except for its ambiguous
historical overtones—wasn't Robespierre called the "people's advocate"?) But who better to conduct a defense than a professional
lawyer?

A few words about myself, my roots, and my family.

I was born in 1937 in Chita, Siberia. The area east of Lake
Baikal, near China's northern border, is a special part of Russia. The
stockaded jail of Chita has connotations of freedom for Russians, for it
is here that Decembrists pushed wheelbarrows with Siberian ore
during the reign of Nicholas I. A government of the Soviet of Soldiers'
and Cossacks' Deputies was established here after the armed uprising
at the end of 1905. That government lasted only a month. In the early
1920s, Chita became the capital of the Far Eastern Republic.

My paternal grandfather was a railroad man, an engine driver.
My father followed in his footsteps and later on he graduated from a
railway institute. His studies were interrupted by fighting against
counterrevolutionaries in Central Asia, and by various agricultural

campaigns. He made his way in life between drawing board and revolver, between revolver and sowing machine.

The family received its first shock in 1939 when my grandfather, an old party member and an active participant in the revolution, was arrested.

Soon, war broke out, and my father left for the front. My mother earned 300 rubles a month; a loaf of bread cost 100 rubles at the market.

I may not have been born into the intelligentsia, but our family had some distinctive features that could be traced to my paternal grandmother. She was Czech by nationality; knew Czech, Polish, and German; and had an innate intellectual streak. We were brought up under her tutelage to address our mother and father with a formality that smacked of the old regime. This somewhat unusual and dated respectful address allowed our family to maintain a saving distance under cramped home conditions. There was no lack of vital intimacy, but along with it there was what I would call a "respectable," and respectful, distance.

My first taste of real culture, however, came only when I enrolled at Leningrad University. I am grateful to my professors, genuine Russian intellectuals who managed to keep intact the highest moral qualities and culture throughout the Stalin years.

I graduated with honors and was sent by the university placement board to work in Stavropol Territory. (I didn't cross paths with Mikhail Gorbachev, although he was there at the time.) I completed a postgraduate course at Leningrad University and settled in Leningrad, the "cradle of three revolutions" where on Senate Square, on December 14, 1825, the Tsar's cannons suppressed the first attempt to establish Russian parliamentarianism.

It's a cradle where the diapers haven't been changed for far too long, I might add.

3

Row Seven, Seat Twenty-one

Every cook should learn how to run the state.

Vladimir Lenin

"You called a plumber?"
"Yes, thank you very much for coming. As you can see, there's a leak in the bathroom. We're using a basin to collect water in the toilet. There is a real deluge in the kitchen every night; water drips from the ceiling in the bedroom. . . ."
"I see . . . the system has to be changed."
"Will it cost much?"
"Who said anything about money? I said the *whole system has to be changed*."

A mid-70s joke

The preliminary activities of the First Congress of People's Deputies of the USSR actually got started several days before its official opening on May 25, 1989.

I landed in Moscow for the opening fresh from witnessing the three-million-strong May 21 demonstration that had rocked Beijing and the whole of China, a prelude to bloody events.

I'd never seen anything like it. As we drove from the Soviet Embassy to the Beijing airport on May 22, the road was blocked in several places by barricades made of trucks and concrete blocks. Students and other civilians stood in front of them, picketing. They were wary and watchful, but when they saw that our car had diplomatic plates, Soviet ones to boot, they let us through.

Mikhail Gorbachev was also in China at the time. There were rumors that I was in his entourage. To certain people, this explained why for several days in a row I was given the floor at the Congress, allowed to speak from the rostrum and from microphones installed in the hall. At the risk of disappointing some readers, before the Congress, I'd seen Gorbachev only on a TV screen. I'd been invited to China by a branch of the Chinese Academy of Sciences to look into their experiments with free economic zones and the prospects of their cooperation with Leningrad. My trip began before Mikhail Gorbachev's visit, and ended after it. In any case, we couldn't have met; I was in Shenyang, in the far northeast of China, for most of my visit, while Gorbachev was conducting his talks in Beijing.

Upon arriving in Moscow, I learned that preparations for the Congress were already well underway. We were told that before the Congress, Russia's deputies would meet with the republic's party and government leaders.

The meeting took place on May 23 in the building of the Council of Ministers of the Russian Federation. The old-line apparatchik who was to chair the session lasted only a few minutes. He was utterly unable to control the fractious forum! Accustomed to dealing exclusively with automatons, he hadn't the faintest idea how to handle dissent and the shower of spontaneous questions we pelted him with.

Gorbachev promptly assessed the situation and took over the chair.

After a few words about the significance of the Congress for the country, he opened the floor to questions. We asked him how he expected the Congress to proceed, what we were to discuss, and how we would decide organizational and procedural questions.

My first direct contact with Gorbachev began when I asked how he, as the head of the party and the state visualized relations between the party and ourselves, the people's deputies. I recalled with trepidation a vivid memory of the Smolny Institute meeting where the head of the Leningrad party committee had tried to "instruct" the people's deputies about how to behave.

But Gorbachev's reply was perfect, without a hint of hostility or irritation:

"Everything will be decided by the Congress," he assured us. "We do not intend to decide matters for you, comrades, still less to exert pressure."

As I listened to Gorbachev I became acutely aware of his charisma, which has a hypnotic effect. Right then and there I understood his fabulous rise to power.

By the following year, Gorbachev's allure would be tarnished, and he himself would be less forthcoming. The stress would be evident. But I, too, would find myself changed, less given to smiles and joking. As for Gorbachev, his change in demeanor took place before our very eyes.

But the most striking pre-Congress episode, in my view, was the meeting introducing the new deputies to the old party leadership (in fact, the entire Politburo). This took place two days before the Congress began, in the long, dimly lit hall of the Grand Kremlin Palace, where the people's deputies of Russia today hold their sessions. Along with those party members invited to the meeting, surprisingly the door was left open to non-party deputies. Andrei Sakharov and Ales Adamovich were even given the floor.

Once again we deputies were impressed by Gorbachev's openness, goodwill and, most important, helpful attitude in his conduct of this meeting which stood in such sharp contrast to the grimly constrained air of most of the other Politburo members, who appeared so out of place, strangers in that hall. None of them uttered a word. Silent, distracted, they seemed to be there against their will.

During the meeting we were informed of the results of the plenary session of the Party Central Committee which had been held before our arrival. Recommendations, we were told, had been made on appointments to several top state posts. And, predictably, they were all bureaucratically self-serving. I was particularly appalled at the proposed candidates for chairman of the Supreme Court and the constitutional oversight committee. The Central Committee's nominee for the country's highest judicial post was an unknown party hack with no legal track record who'd worked as chairman of the Moscow city court for a few months, and before that as a civil magistrate. The deputy sitting next to me, also a lawyer, clarified matters: The nominee, he observed, was closely related to a former member of the Politburo. The old guard was clutching at power, seeking to insure itself, "legally" now, against impending difficulties.

I asked to speak. Probably because no one recognized the name of an obscure law professor from Leningrad, I was one of the first to be given the floor. My dream of ten years ago had come true. Standing on the rostrum for the first time, for some reason, I was neither shy nor nervous. I said everything I wanted to say, offering not entirely flattering comments about Prime Minister Nikolai Ryzhkov, who had been nominated as Chairman of the USSR Council of Ministers; a gentle and intelligent man who would have been fit to head the cabinet of any country except ours, being as it was torn to shreds from within. I pointed out that the government he headed, far from ameliorating the internal crisis, fueled it by persistently violating our country's laws. I mentioned specific examples of the Ryzhkov government's flouting of the laws regarding state enterprises and cooperatives, arguing that such a government had no right to remain in power. This conduct only gave license to legal nihilism.

I named several lawyers, well-known at home and abroad, who'd be suitable candidates for chairman of the Supreme Court. In America or France, I said, the equivalent post goes to individuals who command undisputed authority and reknown as scholars, and who give evidence of superior moral character. I asked for a show of hands from the several dozen lawyers in the hall who could attest to the nominee's stature as a legal authority. Not a single hand was raised.

Nor, I argued, was a former local party committee secretary with a mere technical education an appropriate candidate for the crucial job of chairman of the constitutional oversight committee. If we entrusted this vital function to a non-lawyer, we'd opt for laws to be observed "in a Party spirit," that is, based on the Politburo's latest decision, not on constitutional and other legal bases. I had nothing personal against the nominee, but a person not versed in legal matters would have, at best, paralyzed constitutional oversight.

"Would we, I asked, ever choose competence over privilege?" I asked, or rather demanded, that the party leadership learn to live *within* the law.

This simple idea quickly became my mantra in speeches at the Congress, in the Supreme Soviet and elsewhere. But, the Politburo members heard me out in dead silence.

I was handing Gorbachev back his own words about the necessity of a law-governed state. And, to my surprise, I garnered instant support from other deputies, lawyers and non-lawyers alike.

All the proposed nominations, with the exception of Ryzhkov's, were rejected. On May 27, with the First Congress of People's Deputies already underway, the Politburo, in an unprecedented move, convened a new plenary session of the Central Committee. The Congress was offered a new slate of candidates. And I saw that my efforts in parliament could bring tangible results. My electioneering at the subway station hadn't been in vain, after all. I could look my electors straight in the eye. There was hope, it seemed, for productive work to change the country's political system and atmosphere.

The most important words spoken at that meeting were Gorbachev's, specifically his declaration that the party leadership did not intend to give any instructions to communist deputies or to pressure them on grounds of party discipline.

It was clear to everyone that those gathered in the Congress hall were not an obedient flock. Nor were those sitting in the Congress presidium any longer a priesthood incontestable in their wisdom.

The first personal reaction to my speech came from Yuri Chernichenko, who welcomed me as a kindred soul. I was introduced to Ales Adamovich, and to Andrei Sakharov. Attempts were already being made by party loyalists to "drown" Sakharov in applause and hound him from the rostrum. Naively, I tried to persuade Sakharov to pay no heed to the unparliamentary passions of the apparatchiks.

But Sakharov seemed to ignore my words. He began talking about something else, some ordinary, trivial matter. I didn't yet know that Sakharov generally reacted to assessments of his ideas and actions with the utmost dispassion. He alone knew what was going on in his soul. The secret of Sakharov's invulnerability, I came to believe, was the lucid scientist's mind which transcended praise or abuse, and the self-knowledge of a character that holds itself to such strict account that outside words have little weight or meaning. In this, he harked back to the stoic Russian saints such as Sergy of Radonezh and Serafim of Sarov.

In his first speech from the Kremlin rostrum, Sakharov talked about deputies' responsibilities to the people—something we ourselves hadn't yet grasped—about decrees, and about power. The position of the Communist Party in society, he insisted, must be changed. It must tolerate dissent. Sakharov exposed no one, offended no one, and mentioned no names. He spoke about democracy in general and its principles and rights, which touched the most sensitive nerve of the system and aroused unconcealed fury in the hardline part of the audience. But oddly, my own references to specific individuals—I had named names—and my protest against the decisions of the plenary meeting of the Central Committee were supported by these same people. Why did they now give such a hostile reception to Sakharov's theoretical, at times quite abstract, analysis? Eventually, I came to the provisional conclusion that inner dissatisfactions with the Central Committee's policy was already ripening in local party functionaries' souls. They didn't yet dare launch an open counteroffensive, but they were delighted with the unknown daredevil who had the gall to take on the Moscow authorities. They probably missed the gist of my statement in a haze of vengeful euphoria, thinking: "Now you've got what you deserve! Here's the fruit of your perestroika!"

Sakharov, the writer Daniil Granin, Adamovich, and several of my professional colleagues (that is, lawyers) from various parts of the country that day made it clear that unquestioning indulgence of the nomenklatura's existence at the expense of society was over as far as we were concerned. Words were being heard in the holy of holies of Kremlin power that only yesterday would have earned the speaker a term in a labor camp or incarceration in a mental asylum.

The confrontation heated up at a meeting of delegation representatives at the Supreme Soviet the next day. I'd been sent by the Leningrad delegation. Gorbachev acted again as chairman, with Anatoly Lukyanov beside him. Everything seemed designed to demonstrate that this time we were meeting and talking not with party bosses, but with top *state* officials—this, although the chairman was the same, and so were many of the other faces.

The meeting dealt mainly with organizational matters. The speakers, myself included, stayed away from more fundamental political issues. But it was scarcely an anticlimax: on the contrary, an intriguing scene of strategic procedural struggle ensued. Should we start with reports by the government and Gorbachev, or should elections be the first item on the agenda? I seconded a proposal that Gorbachev's report be omitted since he'd been elected chairman of the Supreme Soviet presidium only three months earlier and had nothing to account for. The government, I noted, should be heard. The proposal was adopted.

As I mentioned before, I met scores of interesting people, fellow deputies flung together, during these days. I met stage directors Oleg Yefremov and Mark Zakharov in between sessions. I found myself at the same cafeteria table as one of my favorite Lithuanian actors, Regimantas Adomaitis. Another well-known Lithuanian actor, Donatas Banionis, was also sitting along with us. Maybe I ought to start collecting autographs, I said to myself.

I also got to know some well-known Leningraders better—Daniil Granin, the eminent scholar Dmitri Likhachev, and Holy Metropolitan of Leningrad and Novgorod, Alexei—the future Patriarch of Moscow and All Russia.

My acquaintance with Likhachev had an inauspicious beginning. Pride, as the saying goes, goeth before a fall. A fellow Leningrad deputy suggested that I get my photograph taken with Likhachev as a memento of the occasion. I actually marched up to the distinguished elderly scholar with this absurd suggestion, and he gave me a look that made me want to sink through the floor of the Palace of Congresses. That look spoke volumes: the wise, ironical smile; the perplexity (*What does he want with it?*), and something more; something that couldn't be reduced to words.

A live spectator gets an entirely different impression from someone watching congressional sessions on television. What I saw on TV in the evenings didn't look at all like what I witnessed earlier in the Congress hall.

The Congress was hard work from the very first day. Legal impasses arose immediately. Ways had to be found out of the procedural maze. Oddly, I discovered I had a penchant for this, succeeding several times in such maneuvers. I was seated near a microphone in the seventh row, seat No. twenty-one, and when I waved my deputy's card over my head, the chairman was hard put to overlook me.

Yeltsin

A highlight of the First Congress was the election of Boris Yeltsin, like myself a people's deputy, to the Supreme Soviet. He had previously been the Moscow party chief.

Yeltsin lost in the first round, but this was predictable; he was the only candidate nominated for the Soviet of Nationalities on an "alternative" list and he stood virtually no chance of success. The apparat had done their homework and expended a great deal of effort explaining why *certain people* should be voted *off* the ballot.

When it became clear that Yeltsin had lost his bid, Alexei Kazannik stood up and announced in his melodious Siberian accent that he was prepared to withdraw on condition that his mandate be turned over to Yeltsin. Some members of the audience applauded; others protested. Gorbachev, who must have been aware of the legal ambiguity of the situation, recognized me as soon as I raised my deputy's card.

According to existing legislation and parliamentary practice, I said, withdrawal of one's candidacy must be unconditional. You couldn't cede your position to someone else. Deputy Kazannik could not lay down any conditions to the Congress if he didn't intend to work in the Supreme Soviet.

Rightist deputies, satisfied with this development, began to smile, while the leftists tensed. I glimpsed Kazannik looking perplexed, and Yeltsin, inscrutable as ever under stress. I said I understood clearly that deputy Kazannik wasn't withdrawing, but ceding the field to allow Yeltsin to enter the Supreme Soviet. To effectuate this, we could pass a decision of a purely procedural nature, giving no specific names. Let the post rejected by a deputy elected to the Supreme Soviet be filled automatically by the candidate who had received the greatest number of votes among those who'd failed to be elected. Or, in this case, Yeltsin.

A legal solution had been found which infringed neither the law nor justice. The Congress accepted this solution, and Kazannik relinquished his place in the Supreme Soviet unconditionally. It was filled automatically by Yeltsin. Subsequent developments proved this to have been a wise step. The Muscovites who had elected Boris Yeltsin as people's deputy were satisfied, and the tension in the city was eased. We could get on with our work and preserve hope that a sensible way out would be found in the event of another parliamentary impasse.

I must point out, however, that when the six-volume transcript of the First Congress was published, Volume One contained the following entry: "Adoption of an application by Deputy A. I. Kazannik to renounce his powers as a deputy in the Supreme Soviet of the USSR in favor of deputy B. N. Yeltsin."

It's hard to be a lawyer in a lawless state!

I first met Boris Yeltsin that June at a meeting held at the close

of the First Congress at Dom Kino.* Democratic deputies gathered
to declare organized opposition to the obviously complacent majority.
We were greeted by a chorus of boos from right-wing deputies who
saw us as ideologically off-track. The Soviet parliament had never
before faced a living, breathing opposition, and even the centrists
were unsettled by our action. On a hot June day, we celebrated
Pushkin's birthday by declaring the formation of the Inter-Regional
Group of Deputies.

Yeltsin was elected a co-chairman of the "interregionals," while
I was offered a place on the coordinating committee of our parliamentary group. From the outset, my relationship with Yeltsin was
complex. I sensed mistrust and wariness on his part and responded in
kind. I was put off by Yeltsin's speeches at the Congress and at
Moscow meetings. In my view, his populist vigor at times ran rough-
shod over common sense, a defect in a politician.

During a short parliamentary trip to Greece, our attitudes un-
derwent a change. Over the course of three days' stay in the same
hotel, our mutual wariness almost disappeared. Later, we'd meet
every day at session of the Supreme Soviet, and our positions would
grow steadily closer, even as we remained frequently critical of each
other's statements. By the time a year had passed, we learned that no
fundamental disagreements of principle divided us.

Distrust of those who differ from one in social background and
temperament is a real problem in politics. For a long time, I saw
Yeltsin as just another party hack, a product of the system. He might
be democratically minded, and he'd been cut off by the system, but
to me he remained in its mold. Yeltsin in turn saw me as a representative of Soviet academia, known for its conformism, servility, and
weakness. Working together was the only way to bring such individuals closer. That is what happened, although the process was by no
means smooth. Yeltsin shared Gorbachev's well-known touchiness;
without warning, he would put credence in some rumor (for instance,
when he said in Leningrad that "according to his information" Sobchak had left the Inter-Regional Group).

But, to get back to the Congress, I had intended to take part in
the debates on Gorbachev's opening report and was raring to propose
necessary changes in the economic and political system, above all,
about the conclusion of a new Union treaty on confederate principles.
I wanted to say that our republics were equal, all right—equal in their

* The Filmmakers' Guild Hall.

lack of rights and genuine independence. The future confederative system must operate on an "equal but different" principle.

Each republic had its national and economic idiosyncrasies. Estonia and Turkmenia, Byelorussia and Kirghizia, couldn't be made the "same" by administrative fiat. I would point out that even the tsarist government of the Russia which we were so quick to call a "prison of nations" actually took this reality into account, granting special status to Poland, Finland, and the Bukhara Emirate.

Unfortunately, I wasn't given the floor. It was one thing to allow me to provide useful legal references, brief and harmless to the presidium, quite another to permit a political statement of an independent stance. I realized that the authorities had taken note of me. There was no point in protesting, so I accepted the tacitly proferred role of a legal advisor at the Congress.

Suddenly, I found myself being greeted on the street by strangers. I was never alone, and could hardly take a step without having to say hello to just about everyone I saw. This was especially true in Leningrad, where it took an hour to get from home to the university by tram, subway, and trolley.

Today, when I read articles by muckraking journalists who claim that the Congress was stage managed from start to finish by Mikhail Gorbachev according to his preplanned scenario, I'm amazed at their blind prejudice. People accustomed to tidy schemes seem to shut their eyes when faced with the ineluctable struggle between life and dogma.

Certainly, Gorbachev had a scenario in mind, but budding democracy scored a victory as the script of the Congress was revised in the process. Gorbachev had guts and intuition enough to follow the course of developments and adopt creative, rather than predetermined, decisions.

No one could have foreseen the circumstances surrounding Boris Yeltsin's election, the effects on the democratic deputies of the events in Tbilisi, or the brinksman-like behavior of the Moscow, Baltic, or Armenian delegations. No one knew the real balance of forces beforehand. To substitute stage managing for what actually went on is to ascribe to Gorbachev the dubious gifts of a Stalin-like "genius of all times and people."

Gorbachev, in fact, was thrust smack into the midst of a parliamentary struggle. Whenever he did try to influence the work of the Congress, it only aggravated the situation. Yeltsin grew sullen, ready to explode; the Baltic deputies demonstratively stomped out of the hall; and furious right-wing deputies took off on Gorbachev.

What with the democrats' legislative initiatives, the formation of the commission to investigate the deaths in Tbilisi, and other direct assaults on their historically entrenched monopoly on power, the conservatives had no option but to try to run the ship of parliament aground.

Their blow, when it came, was low—and telling. For several minutes, the audience became a mob of crazed hecklers, a massed wave of ignorance and frenzy. And facing this raging force was Andrei Sakharov.

Sakharov scarcely blinked an eyelash during public scourgings. For years, he'd fought against the system. He had its number. He knew how it molded people who were deceived by it or were willing to serve it. He could endure equally well a friend's betrayal and nationwide abuse. The very opportunity to fight made him invulnerable. The temporal form of the struggle might change, but it was always a confrontation between humanity and falsehood, spirit poised against baseness and fear. But this time conservatives would challenge him to the hilt.

See It Now

June 2, 1989. Ninth day of the First Congress of People's Deputies.
In the morning, leaflets appeared in the lobby of the Palace of Congresses. In an interview with the Canadian newspaper *Ottawa Citizen*, Sakharov had said that during the Afghan war, Soviet helicopters fired at surrounded Soviet soldiers to prevent them from surrendering to the enemy.

The rostrum that day was first given to Sergei Chervonopisky, first secretary of the Cherkassk (Ukraine) City Komsomol (Young Communist League) Committee and deputy from the USSR Komsomol. He dwelled at length on Komsomol problems, then on the Afghan war, in which he lost both legs. He called the war "controversial" and rightly demanded that the country's leadership give a political accounting. He then turned to the subject of military-patriotic clubs for teenagers, saying in the official transcript:

> In our small town . . . we have about fifteen clubs which are attended by eight hundred young men. Activities in the clubs are led by former

internationalist fighters [i.e., Afghan veterans—ed.]. The clubs are engaged not—as certain people accuse us—in the production of 'cannon fodder,' but in the training of physically fit and psychologically steeled citizens of our socialist Motherland, ready for any hardships. . . .

It's not quite clear what he meant by "psychologically steeled" or what really went on in the clubs. Chervonopisky went on to condemn "stingy" bureaucrats who wouldn't allocate better quarters for the clubs, and suddenly took off on "politicos from Georgia and the Baltic republics" who had "been training storm-trooper units." He mentioned Tbilisi and called it a "tragedy," but gave the word an odd twist:

I cannot yet give a definite opinion in connection with this recent, clearly shameful provocation, because I still have certain doubts about some of its aspects. The paratroop regiment from Kirovabad which was mentioned here was one of the last to leave Afghanistan at the end of this controversial war. I am convinced that the boys who saved Afghan women and children in the midst of battle could never become murderers in a punitive force. . . .

So, the Tbilisi tragedy was an "anti-military provocation"? (As if paratroopers, and not Georgian women, had died in the square in front of the Government House!) And those who disagreed were "training storm-trooper units."

"We are seriously disturbed by the unprecedented baiting of the Soviet Army by the mass media." (*Applause.*)

Chervonopisky excoriated the "intrepid reporters from the *Vzglyad* TV program" for their "malicious mockery" of the army. Finally, he got to his main points and read an appeal to the presidium of the Congress from a group of paratroop officers. It was devoted in its entirety to Andrei Sakharov and "his ilk" and it ended with what sounded like both a vow and a threat: "The Congress delegates must know that paratroopers . . . will continue to defend securely the interests of our multinational Motherland."

He was interrupted several times by thunderous applause. Inspired by the support, the speaker turned from Sakharov to Gorbachev. The latter wasn't mentioned by name, but one could hardly misunderstand the reference:

More than eighty percent of this audience are communists. Many of them have already spoken. But in none of the speeches, including the report, was the word "communism" even mentioned. I am a convinced opponent of sloganeering and window dressing, but today I will proclaim three words for which, I believe, we all without exception must fight. These words are: State, Motherland, Communism. (*Applause. The deputies rise.*)

I felt some powerful force propelling me up out of my seat, compelling me to join the standing ovation. I grabbed the armrests and cast a glance at my neighbors. On my left was academician Igor Spassky, on my right, Holy Metropolitan Alexei of Leningrad and Novgorod. The three of us managed not to rise, not to succumb to the mass hysteria. I remembered that feeling from my army service, marching to a military band. But that was only a parade. Here, it was more like a battle. (Perhaps it was only owing to the prayer of our future patriarch that we managed to remain seated.)

State, Motherland, Communism

This triple formula mirrored the ideological prescription of the emperor Nicholas I: *Orthodoxy, Autocracy, Populism.* Chervonopisky was leaving the podium on crutches. A few minutes earlier, the disabled veteran was an unknown functionary. His speech made him a national celebrity.

Sakharov rose from his seat. He seemed bewildered. As he walked to the rostrum, his mien reflected uncharacteristic uncertainty about what he was going to say. He managed to get out the words: "Least of all I . . ." (there was an avalanche of noise from the audience) ". . . wished to insult the Soviet Army. . . ." He spoke haltingly, with long pauses between words. Each word seemed like a heavy stone raised from his chest. He was short of breath:

> I have deep respect for the Soviet Army, for the Soviet soldier who defended our homeland in the Great Patriotic War. Nor do I wish to insult the soldier who shed blood and heroically carried out orders during the Afghan war. . . .

How to respond to a disabled veteran of Afghanistan?—a man who'd earned the right to say: *you* who sat it out in the rear have no right to challenge those of us who endured the gore and horror of the Afghan massacre, let alone to defile the memory of the dead with your conjectures. You weren't there, you didn't see what we saw and suffered through.

> I am not talking about that. I wanted to say that the Afghan war itself was a criminal adventure started by nobody knows who, and nobody

knows who bears the responsibility for this immense crime against the Motherland. This crime has taken the lives of nearly a million Afghans; a war of extermination was waged against an entire nation, and a million people have died. This weighs on us as a terrible sin, a terrible reproach. We must wash off this shame, which brands our leadership who committed this act of aggression against the people, against the army. This is what I want to say. (*Noise in the hall.*)

Did Sakharov realize that his words were falling on deaf ears? A bit later, after the passions subsided, I polled the deputies, asking them if they'd have behaved the same way after Chervonopisky had spoken had Chervonopisky not been a double amputee. All twenty or so of those whom I questioned said something like: "Oh no, it would have been different." *After* the event, they had some shame. Earlier, they'd been oblivious to the nasty game they were being sucked into by this crucifixion's organizers, unaware how accurately the apparatchiks had gauged people's emotions. The absence of elementary political culture among the deputies was shocking. But Sakharov tried to hang on:

> I came out against bringing Soviet troops into Afghanistan and was exiled to Gorky as a result. (*Noise in the hall.*) This was the main reason for my punishment, of which I am proud; I am proud of my exile to Gorky as I am of a decoration. . . .

No one was listening. They let him finish in order to crush him, polish him off.

> This is the first thing I wanted to say. The second . . . The subject of the interview was different, as I have already explained in *Komsomolskaya Pravda* . . .

Sakharov was hounded from the rostrum. We'd seen Sakharov the victor descend from the podium with arms raised high over his head. Now we saw a depressed, nearly broken man descending the steps.

But the lynching had only just begun. One after another, the speakers climb up to the rostrum. I couldn't tell if the order of battle had been preplanned; it scarcely seemed necessary. They all sounded the same tune: marshals, teachers, state farm officials. The session's chairman, Anatoly Lukyanov, clearly had no control over the audience. And Gorbachev? He slumped forward with his head propped on his hands, his face half-covered. It was the first time he was unable to stop a chain reaction of hatred. I tried not to look at him.

The only discordant message was a brief remark by a Latvian deputy: "I assure you in good faith that no thought has ever been given to the formation of storm-troop units in any Baltic republic. There haven't been and there won't be any such units!"

But not a single word in defense of Sakharov.

The final blow came from a teacher from the Tashkent region of Uzbekistan, who said: "Comrade Academician, this one action of yours has cancelled out all your previous activity. You have insulted the entire Army, the entire people, all those who have fallen, all who have given their lives. I hereby express the general contempt of you. You should be ashamed!" (*Applause.*)

Only at this point did the chairman seem to wake up and announce a break until 4 P.M.

I promptly searched out Sakharov. I began to offer some words of encouragement and support. I asked him not to take all this to heart, said something about mass hysteria . . . I told him I had no illusion that he in any way needed consolation from the likes of me, he had no need to justify himself. Why didn't he ask Chervonopisky where he'd obtained his "information" about storm troopers in the Baltic republics? You could have demanded proof from Chervonopisky before you responded to his accusations, I told Sakharov. Then they wouldn't have "drowned you in applause."

Sakharov looked askance at me, but said nothing.

Why didn't anyone rise in Sakharov's defense as he was defamed? You could not imagine the sheer force of the audience's hatred. Why didn't I take the floor? At first, because to do this I would have had to rise with the audience, and in so doing, I'd have broken down and lost my identity. And so the first vital seconds of the battle were lost. With the machinery of civic execution set in motion against the great defender of human rights, we could only hope for an early intermission.

Yes, theoretically, it would have been possible to make a dash for the rostrum and perhaps get the floor. But in practice, the inertia that gripped the mind and will made it physically impossible to come up with a coherent rebuttal. Not only because words were meaningless to this audience, but because the physiological terror of the system embedded in the genes of every Soviet person, the systematic destruction of dissidence over the past seventy-five years of our history, paralyzed us with fear. During those minutes, the entire audience breathed the air of "1937"—the date that symbolizes Stalinist terror to us all. The hall was populated not by deputies, but by a mob of servants, and victims, of the instinct of Stalinism. Sakharov, our leader, lost his nerve up on the podium. And so did we, his timid disciples.

Only after the adjournment did others manage to reply both for us, and for Sakharov himself. But the sense of guilt before the memory of Andrei Sakharov will never be erased from my soul.

At the Third Congress, in the spring of 1990, I would feel for myself the merciless onslaught of a wave of hatred and frenzy. Cast out from the heart of the audience, I would walk towards the rostrum repeating to myself the two words: "No justifications! No justifications!" In my mind's eye, I would see the face of the late Andrei Sakharov.

4

The Melancholy Bolsheviks

Ryzhkov, Ligachev, and the Rest

Someone has very wittily and accurately defined the difference
between a Christian . . . and a Communist of today: the former
told his fellow-man: "All that is mine is yours," while the latter
said: "All that is yours is mine."

Mikhail Fonvizin
1849

To me, Lenin is sacred.

Yegor Ligachev
1990

The push to democracy in the Soviet Union, embodied in the
efforts of the People's Congress and the spirit of Andrei Sakharov,
faced little opposition greater than the hydra-like officialdom imposed
throughout our society from the 1930's on. Since then, appointments
to public posts in the Soviet Union have been made behind closed
doors, and always by the higher-ups. A single word, *nomenklatura*, is
the key to the career secrets of the "Order of Sword Bearers," Stalin's
name for the permanent appointees of the Communist Party. The

aura of secrecy contributed to the fear the nomenklatura inspired in the lower ranks. What fueled this mystique? It's not quite accurate to define the nomenklatura simply as a class of high-ranking government officials, Communist Party and industrial bosses. Nomenklatura has deeper roots in our society. Factory shopfloor foremen or state farm field supervisors were hardly "high-ranking officials," but they were to all intents and purposes, members of their professional nomenklaturas, certainly so far as their subordinates were concerned.

Nomenklatura was the very essence of the system. Its roots reached down to the very bottom of society; otherwise, the system would have been unable to search out and elevate to the pinnacles of power the most acceptable "human material." The self-replication of totalitarianism would have been impossible. In a sense, the nomenklatura was democratic, for it would never balk at accepting new members from plebeian backgrounds. Within certain constraints (known only to the nomenklatura), he who "has been naught could become all."

Entrées into the nomenklatura ranged from hereditary succession (there have been whole dynasties of party apparatchiks) to the merely absurd. The director of a major industrial body in Leningrad told me that in the early 1980s, they were told to send a management-level party member for a course at the Higher Party School. Unwilling to relinquish a valuable staff member, they picked a semi-educated troublemaker, an assistant to the technical department chief: might as well get rid of a problem. . . . Well, two years later, the "problem" graduated from the Higher Party School and took up a post at a district party committee. The people there, wondering how to get rid of him, recalled he was a "promoted worker" and awarded him the job of assistant director of his former association. There was nowhere else to put him—he'd become part of the nomenklatura!

Everyone's heard such stories, and until recently they have still been going on, even in the uppermost reaches of government. The unpredictability of appointments and staff reshuffling has been an inherent fact of the nomenklatura's cadre-selection policy, and of the system that devised it. In fact, it's one of the more conspicuous traits of the entire totalitarian system.

The nomenklatura parasitized our society. Its strength lay in a collective freedom from accountability. And yet, the nomenklatura often offered room to professionals valued by the system, such as prominent scientists, engineers, economic managers, and skilled workers. In fact, the system created conditions whereby many professionals could realize their creative capabilities *only* by joining the nomenklatura and professing fidelity to it. This is why, during the years of stagnation, many socially active people who did not share the communist ideology nonetheless joined the party ranks.

The nomenklatura was a caste whose members could commit one blunder after another without fear, because of their immunity from accountability. As the old thinking goes, so long as "one of us" hasn't sinned against the system itself, his comrades-in-power will go so far as to clear him of criminal liability, should this become necessary. The misbehaver will be shifted laterally, without loss of rank. Allegiance to the spirit of the nomenklatura has traditionally been valued above all else.

Nor were the sciences immune from nomenklatura infestation. When the Bolsheviks were finding their feet, they didn't balk at employing the "bourgeois" specialists of the tsarist regime, but under Stalin, these people, with only rare exceptions, were removed from their high posts. Most were shot or swallowed up in the Gulag. The fruits of their skilled labors were carved up among the party functionaries.

In recent years, representatives of many professions have complained of the hordes of untalented and unprofessional people blocking their careers. It's no wonder the system has collapsed and the economy is on the brink of disaster.

There were always exceptions; once in a great while, a party hack shifted to a new pursuit transforms himself into a professional. This requires an unusual personality. That's why Vadim Bakatin, former secretary of the Kemerovo regional party committee, stood out so conspicuously! When he received the post of minister of internal affairs, he reorganized the ministry's apparatus, took bold measures to enhance the legal and social security of militia members, supported the idea of creating municipal militias, and gave more professional latitude to republic-level internal affairs departments. In November 1990, the members of the Supreme Soviet were handed a statement in which Bakatin offered a sound and cogent assessment of the grave situation in the country and suggested his own program for extricating society from its crisis. Several days later, he was removed without explanation from his post. In his statement, he'd asserted that the war on crime would be hopeless unless law enforcement bodies were given the right to bring criminal charges against top-echelon officials. Apparently, the minister himself had no such right.*

ANT: A Detective Story

The first press "revelations" about the illegal sale abroad of Soviet tanks appeared at the beginning of 1990. Ivan Polozkov, first secretary of the Krasnodar party committee, was the chief accuser. The country's Stalinists, flexing the muscle of the nomenklatura, apparently were trying to ease a new candidate into the role of party "iron fist."

For reasons best known to them, the conservatives were willing to sacrifice both a business they themselves had created, and Prime Minister Nikolai Ryzhkov, who had given it his blessing. By dragging that business, ANT,† through the mud, Polozkov transformed himself from a humble provincial into a national hero, a champion of working people's interests. The aim evidently was to discredit Gorbachev while at the same time smearing the whole cooperative movement (care was taken to refer to ANT as a cooperative venture rather than a state-run concern, a swipe at the democrats who were promoting the co-op movement).

The sleight of hand was masterful. I myself suspected nothing. Based on the first wave of articles, the whole affair looked like an example of a good idea being perverted by economic buccaneers.

A Soviet "Deep Throat"

Quite unexpectedly, a people's deputy, someone in whom I have complete trust, suggested that I have a talk with a top official in the central government. I shall not disclose where and how we met, but imagine my opening a fat portfolio and . . .

The opening pages made it clear that the whole initial setup of ANT had involved blatant legal violations. In addition, the concern was buffered with extraordinary privileges: it was exempt not only from customs duties, but even from customs inspection.

There was documentation of negotiations being conducted by

* After the failed coup of August 1991, Bakatin was made head of the KGB—*ed.*
† ANT is the acronym for an apparat-owned tank manufacturer—*ed.*

ANT on the prospective sale of a batch of 500 Soviet fighter planes to a Middle-Eastern country and on potential shipments of enriched uranium pending resale of large quantities of gold and diamonds. The transactions had not yet been formalized, but negotiations were going smoothly. Clearly, there were solid grounds for a parliamentary investigation.

The official collected his papers and nodded a silent goodbye. I realized that it was my job to bring this nasty-smelling case before the Supreme Soviet, or at least the Congress of People's Deputies. Something, indeed, was rotten here.

A letter sent to me by a prominent professor, a Soviet specialist in foreign economic relations whose name I'm not at liberty to reveal, convinced me that I was on the right track. I quote:

> You have been bold enough to raise your voice against the alliance between pseudo-cooperators and government bureaucrats . . . which is taking root as a result of the limited and halfhearted nature of economic reform. In conditions of restricted allocation of commodities (which is all in the hands of ministries), certain people are given the right, having worked minimally or fictitiously on a product, to sell it at contract prices, although the said product has been manufactured from raw materials bought from the state and at state prices. . . . Especially high profits can be reaped by using restricted channels, access to which is provided by relevant departments which control foreign economic relations. Here, one ruble of investment can bring a revenue of several hundred, sometimes several thousand, rubles. . . .
>
> The staff of state-run organizations or associations are salaried workers, like all government employees, who get no additional advantage from the transactions which they help to conduct (apart from occasional trips abroad and bonuses of several hundred rubles). The whole profit goes into the state's pocket.
>
> An ANT-type state-cooperative organization is a different matter. The special thing about it is the right to share out the profits (which run to tens of thousands of percent) among the employees proportionately to their personal contribution to the barter deal.
>
> What could be the price of an export license or permission for a barter transaction which brings tens or hundreds of millions of rubles of profits, which, disguised as pay, could then disappear into the pockets of the "shadow economy" dealers? The ANT was granted such permission, which gave it virtually unlimited opportunities for conducting barter transactions and the unlicensed export of raw materials. . . .
>
> What basic conclusions can be drawn?

The story about tanks being sold to foreign buyers is a smokescreen designed to distract the public eye from the true nature of financial machinations. . . .

The investigation (or, at least that part of it which received press coverage) left in the shadow the channels which had enabled the ANT to get hold of its exclusive privileges, such as licenses and barter permission, and let it engage in profiteering on speculation and middle-man activities.

Reference to vague promises to fill Soviet shops with consumer goods cannot be given much credence. Had the ministry been thinking about improving the consumer market in real earnest, it could have issued licenses and barter permission to ease the influx of consumer imports through separate contracts for consumer goods.

The ANT is in no way a phenomenon of the market economy, but an offspring of the bureaucratic class, who use state-run channels for personal enrichment.

The reason for the emergence of the ANT case lies in the inconsistency and lop-sidedness of reform, whereby the state-run channels of raw materials allocation are being used by the state bureaucracy as sources of personal wealth.

The letter said it all.

I made up my mind to bring the case before the Third Congress of People's Deputies.

However, I was forestalled by Polozkov, who on March 13, 1990, rose before the Congress and charged Deputy Tikhonov and myself with responsibility for the ANT affair as "co-op lobbyists." I think he would have acted differently had he known whose signature stood at the end of the "birth certificate" of the enterprise that had been caught redhanded trying to trade away a few rusting machines of war. I suspect that Polozkov was goaded into making that statement by those who had duped him on the tanks-for-export story.

The following day I took the floor and responded by citing the evidence I had in hand and the signatures affixed by Ryzhkov and his assistants to the documents that gave the green light to the ANT.

I demanded that a parliamentary commission be set up to investigate the affair. I was told, however, that the case would be investigated by the Procurator's Office of the USSR.

Nearly a year went by. Ivan Polozkov had become well-ensconced as head of the Russian Communist Party. Procurator General Sukharev handed in his quiet, if explicable, resignation. There was no mention of scandal. The Procurator's Office was silent. The ANT went on trading, in fact, it grew. So long as Ryzhkov was in place, I concluded, the deputies hadn't any hope of learning anything more.

The debates that went on that March during the Third Congress were instructive, however, as a portrait of our parliamentary etiquette.

I declared that if the government gave the go-ahead to sell surplus production, including surplus defense products, abroad, it was clear who was responsible for the sale of tanks. Ryzhkov claimed that the government never dreamed the merchants would go so far as to deal in weapons. Of course, the documents belied his claims—why exempt the ANT's shipments from customs inspection and require the KGB deputy chairman to give ANT "all necessary assistance," unless it was a military matter, involving the sale of weapons?

Ryzhkov cut a pathetic figure, pleading ignorance and claiming that Sobchak had "smeared" him. It was embarrassing to watch the prime minister of a military superpower whimpering like a child caught misbehaving.

In a civilized country, the cabinet would resign under such allegations. But voluntarily giving up office goes against the grain of our "whimpering Bolsheviks," and society still lacks the political leverage to force them to quit.

I dared to go beyond ANT to talk about "indirect" legal violations, such as when members of the nomenklatura who feared that they might lose in the central regions entered themselves as candidates for people's deputies in remote constituencies. Why should the Supreme Soviet's single seat for the Adygei Autonomous Region be filled by the chairman of the presidium of the RSFSR Supreme Soviet, Vitaly Vorotnikov? Or Russia's premier, Alexander Vlasov, represent the Yakuts in the Union Parliament? Wouldn't it be better if those seats were held by true representatives of those nationalities?

The nomenklatura ignored all but my final words. Party leaders from the two "remote" regions I had mentioned were promptly given the floor to chastise Deputy Sobchak for "his attempt to drive a wedge into the friendship between the Yakut, Adygei and Russian peoples." (They later confided to me in private that my speech had been too "cleverly worded" for them to see what I was getting at.)

Well, so be it.

I'd already had my first serious run-in with Ryzhkov in June, 1989, over the appointment of the chairman of the government commission for foreign economic relations.

I took the floor then during the parliamentary examination of Vladimir Kamentsev's formal appointment—he was already well-ensconced in that position—and gave reasons why such individuals should not be given access to top government posts. In every post he had held, Comrade Kamentsev had made a complete hash of his responsibilities. The ministries he'd had the honor to head both operated with stunning inefficiency. Under Kamentsev, the ministry of foreign economic relations had rendered joint economic activities between Soviet and Western partners virtually impossible, imposing such tortuous rules and regulations that, until very recently, Soviet industrialists still couldn't imagine taking initiatives in trading with industrialized countries. I added that Kamentsev had turned a major national economic department into a bastion of nepotism filled with relatives of the nomenklatura elite and military top brass.

Several indignant deputies rose to defend Kamentsev, but the Supreme Soviet rejected his appointment. The episode seemed over until Nikolai Ryzhkov questioned my veracity and demanded that I name my sources.

I was put on the spot. I had no sources because I wasn't a ministry insider, but Ryzhkov had overlooked the fact that the whole debate was being televised. In the days that followed, I had to start a special file to hold the torrent of letters and messages pouring in from ministry workers. Aware that not every one of that mass of disclosures warranted attention, I checked up on a few of the more solid-looking ones. Matters were just as bad as I'd said.

Not only did I have the "right to remain silent," I later told Ryzhkov, as a People's Deputy, *I* had a right to question *him.*

"Ryzhkov's a People's Deputy, too," yelled someone in the audience.

Under the law, I replied, one deputy couldn't interrogate another, he could only ask questions of people in office. But I offered to answer voluntarily, saying, "If you want me to be more specific . . ." I held up a yellowed 1987 page of *Moskovskaya Pravda,* and quoted a statement it contained by Yeltsin, who that year, had supervised an inspection of ministries that had revealed rampant nepotism. (Yeltsin had handed me the newspaper, apparently realizing that I was in the same boat he'd been in back then.) I added some more recent disclosures, then said that the growing tensions in the country made it advisable for me to stop right there.

I'd done my job. Ryzhkov would have to back off.

For some reason, I had never been invited to join delegations
of Soviet deputies traveling abroad. Not that I minded: when you
wake up every day wondering whether you're in Moscow, Leningrad, or on a train, the idea of foreign travel is just too much. Suddenly, I was informed I was to be part of a team of deputies who
were to visit America in the Fall of 1989. What was going on?
Someone warned me that Ryzhkov was going to try to finagle Kamentsev into his cabinet while I was away. I did my best to let as
many deputies and journalists as possible know that I was deposit-
ing the text of my speech with the Leningrad delegation, and that
they'd read it out loud to the parliament in the event that the issue
of Kamentsev's appointment reemerged.

Kamentsev's candidacy never came up, although Ryzhkov kept
his unappointed deputy in office until winter, when the ANT scandal
broke. Kamentsev's signature was on ANT-related papers, and it was
his ministry which supervised the ANT. He took an early retirement.

Living astride the rest of society, the nomenklatura has always
held only a tenuous grip on reality. The nomenklatura of the 1980s
was getting perilously close to a state of perfect obliviousness. For
example, when the *Moscow News* recently published a list of delica-
cies being supplied to a Leningrad City party headquarters—a time-
honored practice dating from the days during the German blockade,
when leaders received daily deliveries of fresh peaches while citizens
starved —the Party's business manager simply denied the evidence.
We're not accountable, was his stance. This attitude was abundantly
apparent during the early days of the People's Deputies.

The first Congress of People's Deputies signalled a disruption of
the long-established nomenklatura order. Decisions of the Central
Committee, even of the Politburo, no longer were binding.

Times had changed. In the past, the party would make its choice,
the newly appointed minister would just turn in the key to his old
office, and that was that. Now, he had to undergo scrutiny by a
parliamentary committee. There, we witnessed some remarkable
transformations.

Our distinguished visitors didn't seem to have learned a thing.
They'd show up, acting detached and superior, evincing scorn for the
"red-tape" hearing "you democrats" were staging. They would con-
descend to take a seat, checking their watches with an air of busy

importance: "Make it quick, please, I have to chair a meeting in half an hour!"

But then, the deluge of questions would begin. The prospective candidate would turn out to be ignorant of things any rank-and-file engineer—or, for that matter, a college or high school student—would know. As a rule, this was accompanied by complete unwillingness to accept responsibility for problems in their jurisdiction. The minister-to-be forgot his "urgent" meeting and sat before us, an ordinary and very frightened man. And yet, he still did not grasp what was happening, why the committee was making the "utterly absurd decision to recommend that he not be reconfirmed in a post he'd held so long."

The fact began to sink in; these "non-recommendations" constituted a *final* committee verdict. During the First Congress only the minister of railways got through on a third or fourth try, and this only because Ryzhkov and Gorbachev implored the deputies to accept the nomination for the simple reason that there was no other candidate.

About one-third of the aspirants failed to win approval. Some were blocked in committee, the rest in the Supreme Soviet session. This latter stage came as a second blow to the bumbling ministers: those who managed to squeak through committee hearings still faced a stringent examination by the parliament. At times, debates went way past the bounds of parliamentary courtesy.

The nomenklatura appointment system clearly was on its way out, and its stalwarts began to betray the first signs of anxiety. Clearly, they'd have to make a concerted effort to ensure their survival. It took them a while to get rolling, for they'd grown unaccustomed to other than internecine competition. Tried and true apparat techniques had given them some major victories during the First Congress, particularly during the opening days, when the democrats were still disunited. Apparatchiks had been installed as heads of several standing commissions and committees of the Supreme Soviet. Back then, when deputies were still trying to sort out who was who, they tended to accept recommendations from the top.

I still remember the acute feeling of helplessness that overpowered me at the end of one of those sessions. My only desire was to throw in the towel and never come back to that Congress hall again.

But I resisted the desire to hand back my deputy's credentials. The next morning, it was back to battle—eight hours of hard work, eight hours of hope, eight hours of frustration. The worst was the day when chairmen of the standing commissions and committees were elected. I took the floor to give reasons for voting against a list of candidates—only to see each and every one get in.

Nonetheless, the election constituted only a partial victory for the orthodox apparatchiks. The basic spirit of the First Congress militated against the nomenklatura and its principles. The conservatives were smart enough to get the message. The conservative opposition to Gorbachev began to coalesce immediately during the Supreme Soviet session that followed the Congress. Hitherto, the conservatives had presented no organized opposition to Gorbachev. In fact, his policy had suited them in a number of ways; conscious of the inevitability of certain changes, they tried to turn them to their advantage.

The middle echelons of the nomenklatura aspired to the top, and seeing old-timers off increased their own chances of climbing the promotion ladder. So it has always been. On the other hand, there have always been the tenacious *éminences grises* of the system: The Mikhail Suslovs, the Yegor Ligachevs.

Yegor Ligachev

Long before the First Congress, Ligachev was already a notorious figure in Moscow. Since the days of the ill-timed anti-alcohol decree which did so much damage to the country and brought fabulous profits to black-marketeers, Ligachev had carried the banner of a fighter for socialist principles. Cloaked in the garb of an orthodox Marxist, he led the crusade to unseat Yeltsin as Moscow party boss.

Ligachev's ascent to Kremlin power dated back to his days as Central Committee personnel chief under Andropov.

By the late eighties most of Andropov's inner circle were long gone from their posts, but Ligachev hung on, becoming benefactor and "tsar" to many newly appointed regional party bosses.

The personnel connection was the secret of Ligachev's long-standing invulnerability. He had never evinced any particular talent, but in the eyes of the nomenklatura, power is a reasonable substitute for ability. And a flair for the "big lie" is considered a real plus.

In the end, Gorbachev shifted Ligachev from ideology (the usual next step for personnel heads) to agriculture, but even there, Ligachev held on for a good long while.

It is virtually impossible to ruin Soviet agriculture; collectivization and destruction of the peasant's spirit under Stalin already took care of that. Ligachev, however, managed somehow, and his ruinous fidelity to collective and state-farm policy, his attempts to inject billions of rubles into the doomed agricultural command economy, and his reliance on party secretaries and farm chairmen who were swiftly and skillfully throttling private farming in its infancy, are a legacy we'll have to live with for quite some time. How long will it take the once bitten, twice shy farmers to take back the land, and try to overcome the food crisis?

Ligachev, unlike other diehards, was comfortable in front of the TV cameras, chatting about his family and his favorite authors. And so he became the symbol of Marxist orthodoxy, and when the nomenklatura's political comfort was threatened, the orthodox instinctively began to rally around him in fighting perestroika.

What a nomenklatura official dreads most of all is not loss of power, although large doses of power admittedly are quite addictive. He dreads even more the loss of "respect." The moment comes when he finds himself in a paradoxical and absurd situation: he's lost none of his power, but his statements can be challenged by any rank-and-file deputy or newspaper columnists. And worse—they're free to laugh at his words! From a human point of view, I sympathized with their obvious sense of humiliation. It was like pitying a spoiled brat torturing a cat: he's clearly a victim as well as a torturer. Admittedly, one feels sorrier for the cat.

During the 1989 parliament, many of the nomenklatura officials couldn't stand the pressure. More than one hundred upped and resigned "of their own accord" at one Central Committee plenum, clear indication of crisis at the top.

Ligachev had no intention of resigning. To be fair, he was sincerely convinced that he was in the right, and had no idea how absurd his position looked from the outside. Ligachev was no fool. But like Khrushchev, with whom he shared a shrewd peasant wit, he seemed to have a native inability to acquire the knowledge, the social and political cultivation, which would "civilize" him. This may have been a stroke of luck for us—the last thing we needed was *sophisticated* neo-Stalinists.

I was sure Ligachev would be the first to resign following the report of the Tbilisi commission, but someone else took the fall. Apparently, the party apparat was having a hard time finding an adequate replacement for Ligachev. Only when Ivan Polozkov emerged from obscurity were they satisfied that they had their man, and only then was Ligachev finally pensioned off.

There was always the threat of military dictatorship—a "dashing" colonel, perhaps—but despite signs that something of the sort was being considered deep within the nomenklatura, in the summer of 1989, the time was not yet ripe to "put the squeeze" on Gorbachev.

The Constituent Congress of the Russian Communist Party and the Congress of People's Deputies of the RSFSR were held simultaneously in the Kremlin beginning June 19, 1990. I was a delegate to the former.

By a two-thirds majority, Russia's communists voted to send a delegation (led by Gorbachev) to the Congress of People's Deputies to torpedo a proposed decree on depoliticizing Russia's punitive bodies.

It was painfully clear what would happen if Gorbachev proceeded to harass the Congress chaired by Yeltsin. I was afraid, however, that the chairman, Anatoly Lukyanov, was not fully cognizant of the situation. I felt compelled to approach the podium where the presidium members were seated and request a chance to speak.

Lukyanov, a veteran bureaucrat, gestured helplessly: "But I see no reason why . . . the vote's been taken . . ."

I appealed to Gorbachev, who nodded to Lukyanov: "Let him speak."

We've just committed a grave political error, I told the assembly. Sending a deputation to "discipline" Russia's deputies was an announcement to the whole world that our Party's only props were the bayonets of the army, the KGB, and riot squads. I proposed a re-vote.

Lukyanov yielded to pressure. This time, about two-thirds of the delegates voted nay. But, although it had lost another rearguard action, the system didn't give up its hope of reviving the "good old days."

After all, it had plenty to protect. Indeed, apparently a leading exemplar of this movement was "poor" Nikolai Rhyzkov, who reportedly decided to begin the transition to a market economy with himself by buying his state-owned dacha at an absurdly low price.

Later in 1990, when I saw the democratic process slipping and the political leadership backtracking, I felt like reminding Mikhail Gorbachev of his own, oft-repeated words: "There is no alternative to perestroika."

Alas, there remains an alternative—the possibility, be it ever so transitory, of a dictatorship of the nomenklatura.

Left and Right ("Right" and "Left")

I myself experienced the wrath of the political right-wing following the December, 1989 report of the Tbilisi commission, which I chaired. (We are in the habit of using "right-wing" to designate *our* conservatives, that is, the supporters of orthodox Marxism.) I am not the first to note that under communist regimes, the political spectrum is in a sense inverted: in our political language, "left-wing" stands for democrats, i.e., the forces who favor a market economy and civil freedoms, whereas "right-wing" denotes the apparat, the nomenklatura, the military top brass, and national patriots. This division is only natural in our Through-the-Looking-Glass state. Our right-wingers do resemble the West's in the sense that extremes of both totalitarianism and imperialism meet in identical mentalities. That some are communists and others defenders of private property makes little difference. The totalitarianism of the ultra-left is exemplified in figures of Lenin, Stalin, Mao.

This is why national patriots, particularly military top brass and chiefs of the secret services, easily make common cause with communist functionaries. Dogma is dogma. "Cold war hawks" are the same everywhere.

Our right-wing press set out in February of 1990 to present me as a slanderer and secret enemy of the military. As it happened, a naval officer claimed, in the Leningrad newspaper, *Smena*, that I had defiled the Soviet military. Defending my good name was an obligation as a people's deputy: bringing a libel action would not only teach my accuser a lesson, but would also set an example of how to act in a law-based state. The proper step was not to appeal to the Central Committee, as Yegor Ligachev had when special investigators accused him of taking bribes, but to seek protection in a court of justice.

I proceeded to file a complaint against the officer, Admiral Yegor Tomko, who'd accused me, I later learned, not only of anti-military sentiment, but also of "selling myself to the voters." In my capacity as a law professor, I had given a lecture on "Perestroika or Apocalypse," at the Leningrad City Council cultural center. The fees from the audience of several thousand, along with my honorarium, were donated to a fund for the restoration of the ancient Smolenskaye Cemetery, which was in a state of great neglect.

The judge at the district court where I filed the claim seemed bewildered to see a man do what I considered only normal for a citizen of a civilized society. He asked me to leave the documentation with him. I'd be informed of the results after the materials had been examined.

Proceedings were initiated in due course, but the admiral did not bother to show up at either the district or city court sessions. When a special board was sent from Moscow by the Russian court of justice to deal with the case, the admiral declared that Leningrad was not part of Moscow, and he wasn't about to present himself in the courtroom.

As head of a military college, he found ready excuses to be out of town—supervising exercises, attending a party congress—and to send subordinates in his stead to represent him in court. He obviously had no refutation to offer, and was unaccustomed to being held accountable for his words and actions. Before six months were up, however, he was forced to pay damages and apologize.

As a plaintiff, I was satisfied: the court had ruled that I had neither slandered the army, nor "sold myself." Personally, however, the whole affair left behind a sour taste: the nomenklatura's apologies are worth about as much as its crocodile tears—tears which Mayakovsky, the Bard of Bolshevism, never thought he would see.

5

The Tbilisi Syndrome

Lies, Alibis, and Evasions

... This hellish work that we're out to do will be done and is
already being done.

Vladimir Mayakovsky

When the First Congress of People's Deputies was setting up
parliamentary commissions I wanted to take part. The only
question was, which of the three original commissions to join? The
first, on the Molotov-Ribbentrop Pact? The second, looking into the
activities of the special anti-corruption investigative team led by
Gdlyan and Ivanov? Or the third, on the deaths of civilians in Tbilisi
on the eve of the Congress?

The first commission's brief was pretty much cut and dried;
materials relating to 1939–1940 that were beginning to appear in the
Soviet press, and documents that had long been accessible to lawyers
and historians around the world, left no doubt as to how, and by
whom, the pre-World War II fate of the Baltic states had been decided. Despite the importance of a political verdict, and of the Soviet
Union acknowledging the deal made between Stalin and Hilter, I had
no professional or parliamentary interest in investigating what was
common knowledge. Historical revisionism strikes me as irrelevant.

The Soviet occupation of the Baltic states is a fact of history; it can't be replayed or erased. Recognition of the tragedy of those months for both the Baltic peoples and the Soviet Union was another matter, but even this ought to reflect awareness of the political realities of that era.

The investigation of bribery and corruption was of far more interest to me, and I thought my experience as a criminal-court lawyer and my scholarly background would stand me in good stead to explore what had come to be known as the Gdlyan and Ivanov affair. As matters turned out, however, I was unable to join this commission.

When Nikolai Ivanov, a Muscovite, had canvassed in Leningrad in his run for a "territorial" people's deputy seat, I'd made it clear that I opposed his candidacy—not on personal grounds; we were not running against each other, nor were we acquainted—but for the simple reason that a Muscovite's victory would mean the loss of the seat traditionally held by Leningrad in the nationalities council of the Supreme Soviet. Seven of Russia's eleven seats were already held by Muscovites, and we weren't about to make it eight. Nor, quite frankly, was I particularly impressed by Ivanov's campaign platform, which seemed to be overflowing with eclectic populism and political amateurism.

The Congress had nominated me as candidate to all three commissions. I searched out Ivanov and Gdlyan during a break between sessions (as a rule they stuck together) and told them I would decline to be on the commission investigating them, ostensibly for abusing their government-granted authority. If they were vindicated, their opponents would accuse us of collusion (Ivanov and myself were members of the same Leningrad delegation), and, if I came to the conclusion that they were guilty, Gdlyan and Ivanov inevitably would see it as part and parcel of opposition to Ivanov.

Both men accepted my argument.

This left me no choice but to ask to be part of the Tbilisi commission.

Its work started right at the Congress, as the assembly was whipped up into bitterly divisive arguments about the events of the night of April 8th–9th. Several distinguished Georgian deputies launched a broadside attack against Gen. Igor Rodionov, one of the commanders who had been involved in the Tbilisi events.

Battle Stations

The smell of blood in the Georgian city of Tbilisi still hung in the air. Georgia was still numb with shock. Updated reports about poison gas victims continued to come in. The Congress rostrum was fraught with the people's wrath. Gen. Rodionov placed the blame on "extremists" who sent in squads of militants and organized violent resistance to the troops in Tbilisi's central square. According to the general, the women who were killed were being used as live shields by rioters.

Naturally, the Georgian deputies rejected this interpretation. From their perspective, not only did troops attack unarmed civilians, using army shovels and gas to disperse the crowd, they refused even to identify the poison gas, thereby complicating attempts to treat its victims.

At the Congress, and across the country, the tension was heightening, although speeches made by Gorbachev and Lukyanov helped calm things down a little.

Georgian deputies demanded answers from the central authorities. Never mind a commission one deputy said, we know what happened, just tell us who gave the order. . . . It was high time Gorbachev told the Congress the truth.

It seemed a reasonable enough request, considering that special internal troops and an airborne regiment answerable only to Moscow were involved. The order *must* have come from the capital.

The electrified audience awaited the name.

Gorbachev resisted the pressure: The matter required careful study; it concerned the very pillars of our political system. We needed a commission.

But Gorbachev made a dangerous slip—before an audience primed to hear his name confirmed as the one who had issued the order for the Tbilisi crackdown, he said he had returned to Moscow from Britain on April 8, when in fact, his plane landed in the late hours of April 7. He aggravated the situation by asking Lukyanov to read out coded messages which had been sent to Moscow by the head of the Central Committee of the Georgian Communist party. Up until then, Georgia had been sure that Moscow was entirely to blame; now, this bombshell gave evidence that the troops had been sent in response to appeals from panicking Georgian leaders. But word soon got around that Lukyanov omitted the last paragraph of the first cable—in which Georgia's leaders requested aid from Moscow "based on the aforementioned measures." Lukyanov had held the original cable up to the TV cameras, but no one in the Congress hall or the TV audience could have made out the words.

Meanwhile, the Congress rapidly switched the blame to the Georgian leaders. Demands for an immediate answer ceased. The Congress went on to set up a commission, although this, too, was not without incident. The first few proposals for head of the commission were knocked down or declined the job. Names came and went. Finally, a list of members was endorsed on May 31.

The members convened on June 1. The first item on the agenda was to appoint a chairman. I put in my two cents, saying that before we got to work, we also had to draw up a course of action. I proceeded to itemize some questions to be answered, documents to be studied, and people to be interviewed. We were the first parliamentary commission to start work at the Congress, and the Soviet Parliament had no experience with such hearings. A commission member said: "Seeing that Sobchak has a plan, let *him* be chairman." There was general approval.

I tried to decline, saying the responsibility was too great, and proposed Professor Alexander Yakovlev, a noted criminologist whose reputation and juristic experience would be indispensable in a parliamentary investigation.

Yakovlev agreed that the commission ought to be headed by a jurist, but declined to serve and proposed my name again.

Some of the party bosses were not pleased by my appointment, but the commission did not come up against any obstacles at this early stage. The party apparat was still in clear control, and even a troublemaker like myself was no great bother to them.

The commission's members covered a wide range of character, temperament, experience, and outlook. The chairman would have his job cut out for him preventing bickering and dissent.

"Consensus" is new to the Soviet political lexicon. In the past, even the most absurd proposal received "unanimous approval." Now, work had to be organized to allow people with differing experience and political views to reach a "collective" opinion. Insistence on a "minority report" almost invariably leads to discrediting of a group's work. It's a virtual certainty that the conclusions will be contested by some portion of its members. In such cases, the conclusions are normally "taken under advisement"—a euphemism to camouflage the absence of tangible results.

Strange as it may seem, one of our first considerations had to be where we wanted to end up with our investigation. We may not have been able to predict what we would find along the way, but we could aim at producing unbiased results. We decided to head first to Tbilisi and after that return to Moscow, where we planned to interview everyone who was in any way involved in the events of April 9. Were we to begin with Moscow, many of us would have looked at the issue narrowly, through "Moscow eyes." Just as a police investigator starts by inspecting the scene of the crime, our commission set off for Georgia a week and a half after the First Congress adjourned.

Towards the end of the Congress, Gorbachev stopped by to see us. We pelted him with questions. He repeated that he'd been in Britain on the eve of the tragedy. The central authorities had kept him generally informed, but he hadn't been aware of the details until about 10 A.M. on April 9, when news of the tragedy reached him at his dacha (he'd gone there on April 7, straight from a brief meeting at the Moscow airport).

The Supreme Soviet meeting held immediately after the end of the Congress forced us to wait until late June to head to Tbilisi. Most of the commission members were able to make the trip. Gen. Govorov used an army plane, while the rest of us took a commercial flight. We landed late in the evening and were taken to the Georgian Council of Ministers' dacha in a Tbilisi suburb.

Next morning, I called together the commission members and asked them to abstain from private contacts with local friends and acquaintances. That way, no one would be able to say we had succumbed to local pressures (which inevitably would have been exerted).

Our minds made up on this score, we phoned our local acquaintances and friends, who, in an expression of Georgian hospitality had been calling our hotel rooms, and told them we were here on business and couldn't visit—no offense intended. I couldn't speak for anyone else, but certainly my colleagues at Tbilisi University indicated they understood.

We also agreed not to make any trips into the city until our work was done. If a trip became unavoidable, no one would go alone.

These precautions were of course meant to preclude any possibility of provocations or accidents that might cast doubt on our efforts. We abided faithfully by these strictures (not to mention total abstinence from alcohol). It was all work and no play, the only exception being when the film director Eldar Shengelaya, a commission member, took us to his native Alazanskaya Valley to attend the reopening of a newly restored exhibit devoted to his mother, the famous actress Nato Vachnadze.

There we found an ancient mansion, with visitors from nearby villages, an atmosphere of solemnity and light, beautiful songs, and lofty words. We left with the feeling of having brushed up against the very soul of the Georgian people.

When you work without distraction, you lose all sense of time. At 10 A.M. we were driven to Government House for the hearings, which were held in the conference hall of Georgia's Supreme Soviet. At midday, we took an hour and a half for lunch, and then worked through until evening. By 7 or 8 P.M., we returned to our dacha to resume work in private, discussing the results, studying the testimony of witnesses, and making plans for the next day. There were facilities for watching video tapes and films.

Of particular value was a video made by a KGB camera crew, which showed the entire course of the rally and the massacre in front of Government House. We played it over and over, using the chronometer in the corner of the screen to time the events with stopwatch precision. The film ran uninterrupted from 9 P.M. on April 8 to 5 A.M. the next morning, by which time it was all over, the camera swooping over an empty square littered with torn clothes, lost shoes, handbags, and bottles. To give the cameraman his due, he had installed himself expertly in the Artists' Union building opposite Government House, giving himself a perfect view of the square.

We also watched footage filmed by Georgian filmmakers and amateur cameramen. These offered less visual information, although watching it after the KGB film gave me an eerie feeling of having joined the crowd just after the deadly countdown had begun. Except, of course, that I knew what was coming. The camera picked out faces of people in the square displaying the gamut of human emotions. A few moments later, they would all shift to a single expression of horror.

The routine of questioning people was the hardest part of the job. We interviewed the republic's government officials and party leaders—everyone who had been involved in making decisions and sending coded messages. Mainly, however, we were interested in talking to eyewitnesses: city residents, ambulance doctors, churchmen, soldiers, army officers. In search of fresh evidence, we went to paratroopers' barracks (the regiment that had been sent in to disperse the rally), where we were told by the paratroopers that they had been ordered to use army shovels against civilians: they could not disobey their orders. Meanwhile, their superiors denied that shovels were used (an anonymous leaflet circulated at the Second Congress of People's Deputies of the USSR later repeated this denial).

We proceeded to Regiment 8 of the interior troops, the worst-hit victims of their commanders' ineptitude and bungling. We also met with militia members and medical personnel, and individuals from a wide range of professions and political views who had either participated in the rally or been eyewitnesses to the April 9 massacre.

Our next step was to summon members of the Trans-Caucasian Military District, including Gen. Rodionov, who led the crackdown, Gen. Samsonov, the district chief of staff, and others.

We examined all the military papers, coded messages, and directives. Two of us had been given the necessary security clearance to inspect these classified documents. We also studied documents made available to us by the KGB, the Council of Ministers, and the Central Committee of the Georgian party.

We got a clear picture of the mechanics of the tragedy, at least from the Georgian perspective.

It remained to be determined what happened in Moscow. It became apparent to us that Gen. Rodionov acted contrary to a written directive that reflected Minister of Defense Yazov's order stipulating that troops be called in to protect major government and municipal offices. Rodionov was to provide security for the Central Committee building, the municipal airport, and the prison. Instead, he ordered his troops to attack unarmed civilians. What prompted a three-star general to act alone and precipitate a tragedy? Did the Moscow end of the investigation hold the key?

Why? we asked Rodionov in genuine bewilderment. Why had he exceeded his authorization. He was the highest ranking officer in the area, he told us, and had been put in charge of the operation by the Central Committee of the Communist Party of Georgia. As a member of the Central Committee's Politburo, he had no choice but to obey. It was a bizarre bit of logic, especially in light of the fact that throughout the whole period of planning, the first deputy minister of defense, Gen. Konstantin Kochetov, was at his side. Did Kochetov tell Rodionov that he was being put in charge of the operation? Or did Kochetov, too, forget to inform his minister back in Moscow that the Georgian Politburo had decided to alter a ministerial decision? We found it hard to believe that any army in the world would allow such an "interpretation" of an order, but the generals stuck to their story.

Therefore, we could safely conclude that Gen. Rodionov had disobeyed orders. With the blessing of the first deputy minister of defense . . . and with tragic results.

Rodionov would be held accountable as a military officer who had failed to obey orders. (In December, 1989, the Second Congress of People's Deputies would later uphold the parliamentary commission's verdict on the culpability of Rodionov and Kochetov. Neither, however, was forced to face criminal charges.)

EXCERPTS FROM THE TRANSCRIPT OF THE
COMMISSION'S HEARINGS HELD IN MOSCOW AT THE
USSR CONGRESS OF PEOPLE'S DEPUTIES ON JULY 25,
1989

YAZOV: . . . The Ministry of Defense issued no directives to disperse the demonstration. I gave no such orders. News about the incident reached me after it had happened . . .

SOBCHAK: Did Comrade Rodionov and Comrade Kochetov inform you on the 8th of April about the pending operation to oust the protesters from the square?

YAZOV: The last time I talked to Comrade Rodionov was around 17:00–18:00, after I returned from the Central Committee. That was in the evening of the April 7.

SOBCHAK: What interests us more particularly is April 8, for it was on the 8th that the decision to carry out the operation was made.

YAZOV: It was around 12:00–13:00 on the 8th, after the party activists' conference. He told me that the conference had made certain decisions. There was no talk, however, of their intention to clear the square of the crowd. I can only presume that they decided on this later on.

SOBCHAK: Does this mean you were given no information whatsoever?

YAZOV: That's right.

SOBCHAK: Do you consider Comrade Rodionov's and Kochetov's actions to have been correct?

YAZOV: No, I don't. They should have informed me of their intentions.

SOBCHAK: In any event, they acted within the limits of their powers, did they not?

YAZOV: Well, I do believe that the commander and the first deputy had such powers. No one thought things would go the way they did.

SOBCHAK: I am still interested to hear whether you think that certain rules were broken. Should Rodionov or Kochetov receive some sort of punishment, albeit only disciplinary action, for acting incorrectly and for exceeding their authority? Do the Ministry or yourself personally see any reason for taking any corrective measures? What are your feelings on this issue?

YAZOV: There are misdemeanors and even crimes that have been committed in the name of good intentions. Now, if we look upon the way Rodionov acted in broad national and political terms, we can't say that his purpose was to cause bloodshed. Rodionov's aim was to restore public order.

EXCERPT FROM GEN. RODIONOV'S SPEECH AT THE FIRST CONGRESS OR PEOPLE'S DEPUTIES OF THE USSR

. . . An overwhelming majority of the city's party activists, and most of Georgia's people's deputies, took part in the conference held at 12:00 on April 8. The conference agreed to the Politburo's characterization of the situation in the city as fraught with violence and unpredictable consequences. All measures to restore order and appeals to reason having been exhausted, there remained the extreme measure—that of using force. Yet when extreme measures are taken, most grave consequences may ensue.

What decision did the general transmit to Moscow after he realized that "there remained the extreme measure—that of using force"? Could we put stock in his candor, given that by noon on April 8, he felt that "most grave consequences might ensue"? I have little doubt that Rodionov was merely a puppet in the hands of those who had latched onto the Tbilisi incident as a way of discrediting perestroika. Although the Second Congress of People's Deputies pronounced Rodionov guilty, for his crimes, he was transferred to Moscow and made head of the General Staff's Academy.

We did succeed in provoking one unexpected, and hasty, resignation—that of Viktor Chebrikov, Central Committee secretary and Politburo member, and head of the commission of legal policies. Yegor Ligachev, who had presided over the April 7 Central Committee meeting where, we determined, the decision was made to send troops to Georgia, stayed on; while Chebrikov, who had presided over a second meeting on April 8, took the heat.

On the plane flying back to Moscow, I brooded over that paragraph of coded message omitted at the First Congress of People's Deputies . . . by negligence, or by design?

EXCERPT FROM THE TRANSCRIPT OF THE COMMISSION HEARINGS

YAZOV: . . . Rodionov was up all night moving the crowd out of the square.

SOBCHAK: Do you mean to say that you didn't see any reason at all to call Rodionov to the Ministry and give him a dressing-down?

YAZOV: Rodionov is not like a new addition to a soccer team to be walloped for every false move. For two years Rodionov commanded an army in the Afghan War. I visited him there more than once. I know him to be of a stouthearted and mature nature. Rodionov could not resort to manslaughter. Now that manslaughter has taken place, he can only be blamed for having overlooked something. This doesn't mean, however, that he should be put in the dock.

SOBCHAK: We are not talking of putting anyone in the dock. What we are trying to make clear is the way you reacted as the Minister. . . .

YAZOV: Let me say again that my reaction was one of remorse. I never said 'thank you' to Rodionov; I said: why did you involve yourself in that when it was the business of the Ministry of Internal Affairs? Well, the decision had been made, he was the senior commander in the area. He was the highest in rank. I am trying to tell you that as commander, Comrade Rodionov had the right to assume responsibility for clearing the square. Should the commission deem it necessary that Rodionov or myself are to be made accountable for this, neither Rodionov nor myself will be in a position to evade responsibility, in a moral or in any other sense. Given that troops went into action, we are to a certain extent. . . .

Procedural Problems

All roads now led to Moscow, but how could we make the Politburo members attend our hearings? In the entire history of the party, they had never been made to answer for their actions.

In Moscow, we began by studying documents made available to us by the KGB, the Central Committee, the Council of Ministers, and the ministries of defense and internal affairs.

We had no problem with access. Staff members of various ministries, the members of the Central Committee, and KGB personnel showed up at the hearings when called. But what were we to do about the Politburo, especially Ligachev and Chebrikov?

I tried various channels, including the Central Committee's administrative department and the members' personal secretaries; but to no avail.

A LETTER TO GORBACHEV

Reasoning that the simplest solutions often are the most effective, I sat down and wrote to Gorbachev.

Esteemed Mikhail Sergeyevich,

The Commission which has been set up by the Congress of People's Deputies of the USSR to investigate the Tbilisi events has completed its work. We have studied all the documents and interviewed all the people involved, with the exception of Politburo members and those government officials who took part in the meeting held at the Central Committee on April 7, and who made the decision to send troops to Tbilisi. In the event that the said individuals fail to appear before the Commission within two days, we shall be obliged to discontinue our work, round it off, and indicate in the final statements that the persons in question have evaded the hearings and will, therefore, be liable to all the ensuing political consequences.

I handed this note to Gorbachev during a late July session of the RSFSR Supreme Soviet. Next morning, my phone rang: "Good morning, Anatoly Alexandrovich! Cherbrikov's aide speaking . . ." His boss was ready to get on the line.

Chebrikov introduced himself courteously, said that he had been told that the commission wanted to meet with him, and that he was prepared to comply. We arranged that he appear before the commission three hours later, at 11 A.M.

Fifteen minutes later, the phone rang again. This time, it was Ligachev. After a virtually identical, honeytongued prelude, I suggested that he come in at 2 P.M., or, even better, 2:30. He asked, Why not earlier? I told him we were seeing Chebrikov at eleven, and it might be a lengthy conversation. There was nearly a minute of silence at the other end of the line. Ligachev apparently found it hard to believe that testifying before a parliamentary commission could take that long. But all right, he would be there at half past two. (He ended up having to wait anyway; each of the interviews lasted more than three hours.) This was not the commission's fault. Both men gave imprecise answers, wasting time with irrelevant political generalities in an attempt to avoid specific issues.

According to Ligachev, the April 7 meeting at the premises of the Central Committee was a purely routine "exchange of views." No minutes were kept. If every such meeting received press coverage, he said, the presses would run out of paper. He had gone on leave right after the meeting, and had learned about the incident from the newspapers.

Two things he said stuck in my mind: "I'm confident we'll have a one-party system"; and, "In the long run, it will become imperative for several, or maybe dozens, of individuals—not many—to be isolated, in order to create a quiet and normal life for the rest." Ligachev and his ilk believed they were messengers of supreme truth, and they didn't spurn any means that might have helped them to attain their ends.

From Chebrikov, I recall: "We had delegated certain powers to the local authorities, enabling them to decide what to do."

This was an object lesson in the idea of collective irresponsibility (or "the principle of collective decision-making," to use the language of party functionaries). The roots of the Tbilisi tragedy lay in the system's instinct of self-preservation. On the verge of political collapse, totalitarianism instinctively tried to crank things up to the point where perestroika would have to be curbed. The crucial thing was to unseat its leader if possible, or, at least, to estrange him from the masses. Indeed, although Gorbachev managed to ride out the crisis, a barely visible rift of mistrust opened up between him and the broad democratic front.

Collective irresponsibility made conspiracies bothersome and risky palace revolutions unnecessary.

We eliminated any claims of ethnic violence or attacks on the army before April 9, but established, in the words of General Samsonov, that several times on April 6, beginning at about 18:30 hours, Boris Nikolsky, the Second Secretary of the Georgia Central Committee, ". . . asked me to send troops to restore public order in the city. . . . Around 20:00 hours Yazov called to ask about the situation and told me . . . not to send in troops without his order. At around 20:30 hours Nikolsky called a third time to ask whether I had been given the order. . . ." Nikolsky described the evidence as "inaccurate." He confirmed that he had spoken with both Samsonov and Rodionov on the sixth, but denied any talk with Yazov. Although no minutes were kept at the April 7 meeting, clearly little time was wasted by at least two of the participants, Yazov and Deputy of Internal Affairs Minister Trushin, who dispatched the first troops later that day without informing Premier Rhyzkov of what I know they—and Ligachev—knew was a lethal decision.

We met with Eduard Shevardnadze. His sincere response to our questions made a great impression on us. He told us that the Tbilisi events were a personal tragedy for him. He had arrived in Tbilisi on April 9 and had begun an immediate investigation of the use of poisonous substances. The military kept repeating that none had been used, and it wasn't until medical experts confirmed that some of the victims had been poisoned with virulent chemical agents that the military admitted the use of various brands of Cheryomukha gas, and later of CS gas.

Why did Shevardnadze take the Tbilisi tragedy so much to heart? In my opinion, it was not only because he was a Georgian and a native of Tbilisi. Had Shevardnadze been in Moscow, not London, on April 7, and had he flown to Georgia early on April 8, as Gorbachev suggested, the massacre in front of Government House probably could have been averted. We followed our talks with Shevardnadze with a communiqué addressed to the secretary general.

ANOTHER LETTER TO GORBACHEV:

Esteemed Mikhail Sergeyevich,
     The Commission investigating the Tbilisi events has completed its work, having interviewed all persons concerned and the actual participants in the said events, and having studied all the documents pertaining thereto. We have arrived at certain conclusions and have prepared the final statement, but we would like to meet with you again, so that the Commission is not censured for not having dared to demand explanations from you, and that you will not be blamed for having denied the Commission the opportunity to be given relevant explanations. . . .

Gorbachev agreed. The meeting took place during the Second Congress of People's Deputies. We talked for about an hour. We asked him to explain why he had misstated the date of his return from Britain, and not revealed who had informed him of the situation in Tbilisi, and how. His answers were as straightforward as our questions.

The date was just a "slip of the tongue." It was a routine welcome; there was no Politburo meeting to discuss the situation in Tbilisi. He couldn't even remember who had briefed him ("Was it Chebrikov, or maybe Ligachev?"). It was at the airport that he'd been told that a "provisional" decision had been passed to provide military support to Georgia and to secure strategic sites and government offices. He had immediately suggested that Shevardnadze and Razumovsky fly to Tbilisi; a plane was standing by to take them. But Shevardnadze had phoned Tbilisi and had been told by Dzhumber Patiashvili, the Georgian party chief, that tensions were subsiding, and there was no need for such haste.

Now, look at the military's official report.

Yazov:

Mikhail Sergeyevich arrived from Britain at around 23:30. We were all
out at the airport to meet him. Straight after telling us about his
stopover in Cuba and subsequent visit to Britain, he asked about the
situation at home. He was briefed about what was gong on in Tbilisi.
Comrade Ligachev said: We have received a coded message from Comrade Patiashvili today; what will be your decision? The decision was to
ask Comrades Shevardnadze and Razumovsky to fly there to deal with
the situation locally. In the event that they decided to impose a curfew,
the decision to send in a paratroop regiment and other units to guard
public facilities would have to be confirmed.

Apparently, the officials who met Gorbachev at the airport never
told him that riot police units had already been flown to Tbilisi, or
that paratroopers would be arriving there in a few hours. Gorbachev
consented to send troops to Tbilisi only if Shevardnadze and Razumovsky decided after viewing the situation firsthand to impose a
curfew. Everybody gave a verbal okay. Yazov simply "omitted" to
cancel the already issued order. Moreover, every possible effort was
made to step up preparations for the crackdown and prevent Shevardnadze from going to Georgia.

The reader is invited to examine the further testimony of Chebrikov and draw his own conclusions.

EXCERPT FROM THE TRANSCRIPT

Chebrikov:

We had a conversation at the airport about the measures that were
being taken. Gorbachev's advice was that Comrades Shevardnadze and
Razumovsky should fly to Tbilisi. But they should think it over and
time their mission properly. We got together once again. That was on
the next day, Saturday . . . We weighed the pros and cons. Then we
asked for one more phone call to be put through. And again the reply
was that everything was OK. . . . So, we decided that Comrades Shevardnadze and Razumovsky would not be flying. We kind of postponed
the mission.

The unsuspecting Gorbachev drove to his dacha to relax after his
trip to Cuba and Britain, and Ligachev hurried off on his vacation.

Anatoly Sobchak, at home in his apartment in Leningrad

The 1989 pre-election team: the professor's volunteers

Campaigning for election to the First People's Congress, in March 1989, in
Leningrad

Moscow, June 1989; the First Congress of People's Deputies

Yuri Chernichenko, the prominent political journalist and liberal People's Deputy, who took on right-wing ideologue Yigor Ligachev in a memorably harsh parliamentary debate

Yuri Afanasyev. Historian and founding co-chairman of the Inter-Regional Group of Deputies, he has remained a leading liberal and member of the Democratic Reform Movement. He left the Communist Party in April 1990.

Gavril Popov. Economist and democratic Mayor of Moscow, he, along with other democrats, walked out of the party on July 13, 1990. Popov joined Yeltsin and fellow mayor Sobchak in resisting the August 1991 coup.

Yuri Karyakin. Historian and progressive people's deputy, he grilled Gorbachev at the first post-coup session of Parliament about, among other things, Gorbachev's poor choice of advisors.

Galina Starovoitova, liberal USSR people's deputy, successfully sued *Pravda* for slander when it accused Starovoitova and other "radicals" of producing an artificial food shortage in Moscow in order to foment a counterrevolutionary uprising.

Dmitri Likhachev. The distinguished historian stood beside Sobchak at the anti-coup rally in Leningrad and spoke eloquently in defense of the city he has lived to see reborn as St. Petersburg.

Alexander Yakolev, Gorbachev's close advisor and architect of perestroika, quit the party two days before the August 1991 coup, warning of the danger of imminent military dictatorship and criticizing Gorbachev for kowtowing to reactionary elements.

Eduard Shevardnadze, the distinguished former foreign minister, alerted the world to the possibility of a right-wing Soviet takeover when he resigned his post on December 20, 1990.

Boris Yeltsin left the Communist Party on July 12, 1991. As President of Russia, Yeltsin was the charismatic resistance leader during the August 1991 coup attempt. Sobchak, as mayor of the second-largest city in the Russian republic, met secretly with Yeltsin during the coup (see Epilogue) and continues to work closely with him.

Anatoly Lukyanov, former chairman of the Supreme Soviet, seen on the left, was dismissed from his post for remaining silent in the wake of the coup. He is shown here with Gorbachev and Sobchak.

Sobchak walking down the aisle after addressing the Supreme Soviet

Dzhumber Patishvili, First Secretary of Georgia's Communist Party at the time of the April 1989 Tbilisi attack against civilians. He was removed from this position even before the parliamentary commission headed by Sobchak finished its investigation.

After the murder in Tbilisi by Soviet troops on the night of April 8, 1989, citizens gathered to mourn the dead.

General Igor Rodionov was found guilty by the parliamentary commission and the Congress itself of responsibility for the deaths of civilians in Tbilisi in April 1989, but never faced trial. "Kicked upstairs" by the apparat into an administrative position at the Soviet equivalent of OCS, Rodionov kept a low profile.

Members of the Tbilisi commission. Sobchak is second from left.

Andrei Sakharov, physicist and Nobel Peace Prize winner, was the founding co-chairman of the Inter-Regional Group of Deputies. He died of a heart attack on December 14, 1989, following a grueling session of the Second Congress of People's Deputies.

Sergei Chervonopisky. The disabled Afghan War veteran accused Andrei Sakharov of lack of patriotism and triggered a right-wing and nationalist outburst against Sakharov at the First Congress of People's Deputies.

Session of the Inter-Regional Group of Deputies on December 14, 1989. This photo was taken several hours before the death of Andrei Sakharov *(Right)*.

December 16, 1989, Andrei Sakharov's funeral. Sobchak is visible just left of center.

Sobchak with Gorbachev on July 13, 1990, the day Sobchak joined other democratic leaders (including Gavril Popov and Sergei Stankevich, the mayor and vice-mayor of Moscow) in leaving the party

Meanwhile, the coiled spring would be released, and nothing could be done to stop it.

Silence can be more eloquent than a confession. Let me quote the letter and the attached explanatory note sent to me by Ligachev in October 1989:

Anatoly Alexandrovich,

In connection with the publications of the conclusions of the Georgia Commission concerning the events of April the 9th in Tbilisi, which quoted the findings of the Parliamentary Commission, I thought it would be appropriate to send you herewith the following note.

Yours respectfully,
Ligachev
06-10-89

To A.A. Sobchak, Chairman of the USSR Supreme Soviet Commission for investigating the events of April 9th in Tbilisi.

Esteemed Anatoly Alexandrovich!

I familiarized myself the other day with the final statement of the Georgian SSR Supreme Soviet Commission for investigating the events of April the 9th in Tbilisi, published by the republic's newspaper, *Kommunist* (Sept. 23, 1989).

I think it would be worthwhile bringing the following considerations to your attention.

The writers of the final statement assert that the meeting which took place on April the 7th this year at the CPSU Central Committee premises under the chairmanship of Ligachev "decided to meet the request for military help, advanced by the Central Committee of the Communist Party of Georgia." They further claim that the above-mentioned statement is "corroborated by the findings of the Commission set up by the Congress of People's Deputies of the USSR." In the meantime, as far as I know, the Commission headed by you has not yet made public its findings. . . .

I would like hereby to reaffirm my testimony to the USSR Supreme Soviet Commission (sic). It is true that an exchange of views about the situation in Georgia took place on April the 7th . . .

At the end of the meeting, I pointed out to the participants that the request for troops had not been collectively discussed by Georgia's Central Committee, but had been made verbally by Comrade Patiashvili alone . . . I suggested that we recommend that the Central Committee of the Communist Party discuss the situation with the republic's (Georgia's) government and Communist Party organs . . . I also stressed the importance of using political methods to defuse the conflict, implying that the local authorities must step up efforts to come to terms with the protesters. . . . Regrettably, those crucially important recommendations by the CPSU Central Committee have not been mentioned in the Commission's statement.

Shortly afterwards, the Central Committee of the Communist Party of Georgia sent to Moscow several coded messages (they were read by Anatoly Lukyanov to the Congress of People's Deputies of the USSR). By that time, or more accurately, in the morning of April the 8th, I had already gone on holiday, as planned. . . .

I would like to remind you, that according to the information from Georgia's Communist Party leadership, the Ministry of Internal Affairs and various departments of the CPSU Central Committee, the situation in Tbilisi had by then worsened and dangerous extremism was on the increase.

I entirely disagree with the assertion in the same newspaper by the Georgian Commission, that "the events of April 9th were no secret to the Central leadership, including Ligachev." The country's leadership heard the news about the tragic events after they had taken place. As for me, I can only tell you that I learned about what had happened from a TV broadcast.

Strictly speaking, I did not take part in the decision-making on the Georgian issue, either before or after April 7th.

These are facts. I would request you kindly to familiarize the members of the USSR Supreme Soviet Commission (sic) with this note.

Respectfully,
Yegor Ligachev
10-06-89

Ligachev lied at the commission hearings and in his letter. He failed to say that the relocation of troops began right after the April 7 meeting, and contradicted Samsonov's testimony that there had been a collective discussion of military action in Georgia on April 6. Samsonov had talked with Nikolski and then with Yazov.

He may have confused the Supreme Soviet with the Congress of People's Deputies, but he knew the mechanics of the Tbilisi tragedy better than anyone else. He supervised the fatal decision that led to it (admittedly, it was followed by excesses on the part of the overzealous executors of the order which he might not have foreseen).

As the day of the commission's report was nearing, it was time to draft the final statement and prepare a report to the Congress.

Among the commission's members were world-famous scientists, writers, journalists and generals. But it also included Afghan War veterans who were young, naive, and totally inexperienced in dealing with such matters. These boys sat tongue-tied during the early stages of the investigation, but later became a great help, especially when we went to interview the paratroopers in their barracks to get the truth about April 9. They also brought into the commission's hearings a large group of their comrades-in-arms, residents of Tbilisi who gave us valuable and truthful evidence about the tragic Sunday morning.

At first, it seemed we would never be able to reach a collective opinion. But in the end we became the only one of the commissions set up under the aegis of the Congress whose final statement bore the signatures of *all* its members, without exception.

Could there be any common ground between an army general and a left-wing Popular Front activist? So long as both were busy trying to find the truth and both shouldered equal responsibility for the outcome of their work, they ceased to occupy roles as generals and privates. They were henceforth members of the same crew, on a ship bound for a specific destination.

We were hunting for facts. By checking, rechecking, questioning, getting tough with one another and eventually determining facts as proved, was developed a unified approach. We brushed aside everything that was not, or could not be, proved. When basic conclusions were agreed upon by all of us, we formed the commission's editorial group.

We got out of the city and set up shop in *Izvestia*'s guest house, working fifteen to sixteen hours a day for ten days, arguing over every written word. We rewrote the commission's final statement dozens of times.

We divided the final statement sections among ourselves, and each editorial group member wrote his own part. We then got together and discussed every phrase and every word. A new wording would then be prepared, merely to be discussed again. At that stage we checked on the possible connotations and, like a laundress wringing wet linen, we'd wring out our emotions and ambiguities, review the logic, and polish the style.

I still remember with gratitude both those days and my coworkers, those fine and noble people with whom we prepared the final statement. Even with the anarchy and chaos that dominated our society, the seemingly irreconcilable positions and views, it remained possible to find a common language and achieve mutual understanding—provided, that is, that all the parties were honest and determined to serve the truth and their people. One hoped that our commission would be a model for our society, and its success would hold a promise for the success of the endeavor that took the name perestroika five years before.

At the 28th CPSU Congress in July 1990, when Yegor Ligachev nominated himself for the post of deputy general secretary of the party, I brought up the question of when he had spoken the truth: when he told the commission that there had been no Politburo meeting or when he told the CPSU Central Committee Plenum just the opposite? A tape recording of the July 13 session preserved the style and mood of his answer to my question.

FROM A TAPE OF MY SKIRMISH WITH LIGACHEV

LIGACHEV: Anatoly Alexandrovich, let me answer this question . . .
SOBCHAK: Please do!
LIGACHEV: Let me ask you a question first, Comrade Sobchak! I have the text of your statement in my briefcase over there. Let me tell you one thing: Ligachev said the same thing on both occasions. After all, I would ask those sitting beside me here to say just a few words . . . to confirm that the decisions had been made by all the Politburo members. Under the chairmanship of Mikhail Sergeyevich Gorbachev. Mikhail Sergeyevich, I ask you . . . I can request you as your comrade and as a Communist . . . (noise in the audience). I am sorry, but I was telling you the truth, and nothing but the truth . . . I said then that the decision had been made by a commission of the Politburo comprised of at least three quarters of its members . . . The only reasonable decision . . . I feel myself to be right even now . . . I am very sorry and I apologize to my comrades in Georgia for the tragedy . . . I am saying this from a humane point of view and I deeply regret . . . It will be inside me as long as I live, but we, the Politburo members . . . have nothing to do with the tragic incident. Our position was firm: the situation was to be dealt with using political methods; we brought this home to the then Georgian leadership very clearly . . . Now, why have

I spoken about the Politburo . . . After you, Anatoly Alexandrovich, reported, more or less objectively to the Congress of the People's Deputies, and the newspaper *Izvestia* gave the report coverage, why on earth did you give that interview? . . . I never spoke about that anywhere, but let me mention it in the presence of thousands . . . You gave the interview two weeks later in *Ogonyok* and you wrote . . . let me tell you what you wrote . . . I'll quote, I'll ask for copies to be made of it . . . What did Comrade Sobchak write? No sooner had Comrade Gorbachev left for . . . Where did you go, Mikhail Sergeyevich? Was it Britain? (noise and laughter in the audience). Britain? No sooner . . . than Comrade Ligachev started a . . . assembled a commission and plotted yet another conspiracy behind his and Comrade Ryzhkov's back . . . Something like that. That's what I was objecting to; tell me why do you do such things: you speak softly and carry a big stick, that's what you do! (noise, shouts, and ovation from the audience).

SOBCHAK: I do not aspire . . .

GORBACHEV: Third microphone!

SOBCHAK: . . . to take the post of Deputy General Secretary.

GORBACHEV: Yegor . . .

SOBCHAK: But I declare . . .

GORBACHEV: Third microphone! Third microphone!

SOBCHAK: But I declare that . . .

GORBACHEV: I am asking for the third microphone to be switched on.

VOICE: Turn that mike off! . . .

VOICE AT THE THIRD MICROPHONE: I am Gerasimov, representing the Komi delegation . . .

It was a pity Gorbachev cut short that exchange because Ligachev was about to unfold a third scenario, according to which the decision to send troops to Georgia had been passed not by "a meeting at the Central Committee," and not by "a Politburo meeting,' but by a meeting of some imaginary "commission of the Politburo, comprised of at least three quarters of its members."

It wouldn't have surprised me if the next day this Ligachev-invented "commission" had metamorphosed into a symposium with participation from the Ministry of Defense, or some sort of seminar on military tactics.

As conservative as most of the delegates were, three quarters of those present in the Congress hall that day voted against Ligachev's candidacy. A moderate, Vladimir Ivashko, became deputy general secretary, and Ligachev was pensioned off by his party comrades, to a universal sigh of relief.

6

Investigation as Comedy
The Gdlyan and Ivanov Affair

If there are some people somewhere in this country who
sometimes do not want to live honestly . . .

An example of criticism during the stagnation era

The names of special investigators Telman Gdlyan and Nikolai
Ivanov became known throughout the country after the June
1988, 19th Party Conference. When Vitaly Korotich, editor-in-chief
of *Ogonyok*, handed the party general secretary an envelope with the
names of four corrupt delegates in the silence of a stunned audience,
it seemed that many members of the presidium were craning their
necks to look over Gorbachev's shoulder and find out whether the
envelope contained their fate.

The most incredible rumors swept in waves from the Car-
pathians to Kamchatka. But those who knew how the top echelons of
power operate realized that if the envelope had contained material
about the country's leaders, Korotich wouldn't have made it to the
rostrum.

Their exposé of the party and economic "mafia" in Uzbekistan
hit the country hard. Corruption in the Soviet Union was an old story,
but it still hadn't sunk in that this was the inevitable consequence of

the party monopoly and the nomenklatura's protected regime, until the Gdlyan-Ivanov investigation got people thinking.

According to a Russian fairy tale, the death of Koshchey the Immortal is in the point of a needle, the needle is inside a golden egg, the egg inside a duck, and the duck inside a casket over three seas. Although Koshchey's castle can be reached, the evil old man cannot be slain with the sharpest magic sword, only with that needle.

Our society is too mythologized (and the Marxist utopia made use of this for seven decades) to believe facts and only facts. It seemed that the two heroic investigators had really reached the golden egg over the three seas—only to find it wrenched from their hands at the last moment by Koshchey's servants. Which is why the corruption case, mishandled in the end by Gdlyan and Ivanov, whipped up such a frenzy.

Once upon a Time

The Gdlyan-Ivanov investigatory team was formed under Yuri Andropov, the former KGB head who became the party's general secretary at the end of 1982. This attempt to strike a first blow at corruption and organized crime was not evidence of any democratizing intention; political logic simply demanded that Andropov get rid of the minister of internal affairs and other officials who were obstructing his vision of a strict political regime with everything put "in order." A "landing party" of investigators was sent out to Uzbekistan to explore the multi-billion-ruble cotton case, a financial scandal involving government functionaries.

Konstantin Chernenko, who soon replaced Andropov, didn't— or, more likely, couldn't—curtail the investigation. The team instituted criminal proceedings against a large group of Uzbek party functionaries and leaders of the republic's ministry of internal affairs and its regional departments. People who had been considered untouchable found themselves in the dock.

Official reports about these investigations for a long time were scanty. Information would come out that an area boss had been arrested, or that criminal proceedings had been started against someone else. It became known that several top-ranking generals of the Ministry of Internal Affairs had committed suicide. One could only guess what all this meant.

In 1988, television reports told of the heroic work of the Gdlyan-Ivanov Soviet investigative team in Uzbekistan. Newspapermen were also active. I remember a color photograph in the weekly *Sobesednik* showing heaps of money and gold from the caches of the Uzbek "mafiosi." Next to it you could see the faces of the exhausted investigators who almost had to sleep in their bulletproof vests. The idea of warriors without fear and without reproach, people who risked their lives every minute for the sake of the restoration of social justice and the punishment of criminals, gave them the image of "defenders of the people."

News about attempts on the investigators' lives spread like wildfire. Though nobody knew the circumstances, few doubted that someone was trying to stop these brave men.

For about a year the mass media had only good things to say about the Gdlyan-Ivanov team. The situation changed drastically in the spring of 1989. Ivanov and Gdlyan, campaigning for parliament, began a series of exposés of the apparat in the press and at meetings with voters. The Uzbek case was said to be only a part of a Moscow one. Gdlyan and Ivanov had uncovered corruption in the Kremlin. Procurator General Sukharev moved to bar further investigation, and Gdlyan and Ivanov responded by talking about the "undermining of their case" wherever they could find an audience.

Was the Procurator General out to destroy his own investigators? Why not? Why shouldn't a stock setup of Italian films—lone heroes against the Mafia—be the stuff of real life in our country? After all, these investigators named highly placed officials, including the likes of Yegor Ligachev, as guilty of criminal activity.

Never since the era of Stalin, had investigators taken on such political fat cats. In the 1930s, however, the agencies of repression had been acting on orders from Stalin; Now, action was being taken more or less on the personal initiative of two desperado investigators.

But the laudatory articles and reports were replaced as if on command by "reconsiderations." The investigators were now "revealed" to have violated laws, ignored procedural rules, and accomplished nothing. As for the caches of gold and banknotes found in Ubzekistan, the newspapers explained that most of the ferreting out had been done by KGB personnel; Ivanov and Gdlyan had allegedly appropriated the fruits of other investigators' labors in order to manipulate public sentiment.

But the public didn't buy this line. After these revelations, Gdlyan collected almost three-quarters of the electors' votes in his Moscow ward. In Leningrad, the Muscovite Ivanov won a resounding victory over well-known, popular local candidates. People started calling him "our Yeltsin"; he'd won in a national-territorial ward: and been elected by *all* Leningrad, just as Yeltsin had been elected by *all* Moscow.

In April 1989, the apparat, well aware that its attempts to discredit the investigators had failed, slapped together a commission whose members included well-known and respected lawyers and legal scholars.

At first, the commission's brief was shrouded in mystery, but on the eve of the First Congress the newspapers *Izvestia* and *Pravda* carried full-page articles announcing that a commission of distinguished lawyers and officials had discovered gross legal violations in the actions of the Gdlyan-Ivanov investigatory team. They had advised the USSR Procurator's Office that a thorough investigation was called for.

As a lawyer, I was astounded by the article's revelation that well-known lawyers and the Procurator General (a signatory to the commission's statement) had made use of materials and documents obtained by KGB personnel. In a flagrant violation of Soviet law, these personnel had interfered with and limited the investigative efforts of a team under the direct aegis of the Procurator's Office. It is this office which has ultimate authority over questions of legality, including the activity of state security bodies.

Such practices put us on a direct path to neo-Stalinism.

Why had my scholarly colleagues, with their detailed knowledge of the law, signed such a document?

Gdlyan and Ivanov wasted no time in announcing that the commission had worked behind closed doors and had not deigned to invite them to the hearing.

The struggle against the recalcitrant investigators was obviously taking a serious turn.

Press Report

To add to the investigators' troubles, a 1989 ruling by the Supreme Court of the USSR cancelled the sentence of an Estonian scientist convicted of commercial improprieties, Johannas Hint. Gdlyan had conducted the case. Estonian deputies and the Estonian press also condemned his investigative methods and Gdlyan himself. Proof of current charges against the investigator was conspicuously lacking. Clearly, that's why this case from several years earlier that had no connection with the investigatory team's activity in Uzbekistan had been reactivated.

Hint was the organizer of one of the first entrepreneurial firms in our country. The firm could not operate without infringing the laws of the day when all commercial enterprise was prohibited. It is clear to me as a professional that Hint had to be tried in accordance with the legislation of the moment. He also admitted his guilt at his trial. It was a payment, or more exactly an atonement for a man ten years ahead of his time. Today we are choking with a shortage of entrepreneurial activity in our society while the number of sentences like the one passed in Hint's case ran into the thousands during the '70s. It was absurd to blame Gdlyan for the totalitarian system's failures. Gdlyan, and his fellow law-enforcement workers played by the rules of the system. It was unreasonable to impute guilt to an investigator for going by the book. It certainly looked like a case of revenge from above.

At the First Congress, Gdlyan and Ivanov demanded the floor to justify the work of their team. Other deputies seconded the request, giving the presidium no choice but to accede.

The audience awaited scandal, and its expectations were fulfilled.

It was disheartening to listen to slogans suitable to a mass rally at a session of the Congress of People's Deputies. I was struck by Gdlyan and Ivanov's lack of professionalism. They failed to respond to easily refutable accusations, for instance, criticism for not recording *on the spot* a full description of every hidden valuable unearthed during searches in Uzbekistan. As head of a two-hundred-strong investigatory group, should Ivanov really have ordered an on-site inventory that would have taken months? But it was Ivanov's subordinates who *later* brought out the fact that valuables *were* weighed and sealed on the spot and sent under guard to the KGB or Procurator's Office, where a special commission removed the seals and made the requisite detailed inventory.

Gdlyan and Ivanov ignored these specific accusations. They preferred to hurl accusations about corruption in the Kremlin to reliance on the facts of their own defense. We saw, not professionals who knew the value of proof, nor parliamentarians capable of showing the link between a particular case and general conditions, but street-corner orators, set on appealing over the deputies' heads to millions of TV viewers hanging on their every word.

Everybody knew that the party apparat was corrupt, that bribes were taken. But the clock was running, and the two investigators weren't telling the Congress anything new.

This was, to be blunt about it, populism, an endemic disease of our nascent democracy.

I realize that Gdlyan and Ivanov were in a difficult situation, with the entire official press (including its liberal wing) ranged against them. I knew that the false revelations about them had reached a level where no mercy could be expected, and this aroused my sympathy and a desire to support these brave men. But the two continued to act as though the traditions of the repressive state machine of the '30s still obtained under today's social conditions. It was sadly true that as soon as someone—especially an investigator from the Procurator's Office—publicly branded someone a "criminal," millions of people believed it on the basis of "class awareness," and were ready to tear the accused to pieces.

Had Gdlyan and Ivanov started criminal proceedings against, say, Ligachev, and had their superiors objected to such a legal move, the deputies would have known how to act. Was Gdlyan and Ivanov's failure due to a matter of miscalculation, or unprofessionalism, or lack of civic courage? I was not the one to judge.

It is dangerous for an investigator to play political games with unverified materials from an unresolved case. Think of Dreyfus: justice and law are jeopardized whenever judicial affairs are manipulated to political ends. Gdlyan's and Ivanov's blindness to concrete facts, and their reluctance to provide legal proofs, were sad evidence of our citizens' lack of legal rights.

In this regard our civic consciousness remains deformed by totalitarianism. The *search for enemies* is too ingrained for us to feel secure against the possibility of a relapse into mass psychosis. Gdlyan and Ivanov conducted their election campaigns and public defense right on that perilous borderline.

At the First Congress, I insisted that the commission being set up to deal with the Gdlyan-Ivanov case be called a "commission to investigate corruption in top Party and state bodies." Gdlyan and Ivanov's claims that the Procurator's Office crushed the investigation when it got too close to top officials had to be verified scrupulously.

If the VIPs were *proved* guilty, there would be nothing to prevent their being brought to justice.

A country that eschews judicial procedures in favor of intimidation is liable to be paid back *in kind* rather than *in kindness.* The following were my words.

SOBCHAK AT THE FIRST CONGRESS
OF PEOPLE'S DEPUTIES

We are setting up a parliamentary commission, not a commission to investigate the case of Gdlyan and Ivanov. The parliamentary commission which we are forming will have to be organized anyway, since it was said today that criminal proceedings have been instituted against Comrades Gdlyan and Ivanov. They are people's deputies of the USSR, so we shall have to decide the question of divesting or not divesting them of parliamentary immunity . . .

Second. Why are we forming this commission? I think that such a step is necessary first of all to verify the accusations made by Comrades Gdlyan and Ivanov against government and Party officials. The purpose of the commission's work should be precisely this and not the verification of what infringements, if any, Gdlyan and Ivanov have committed in their activity. (*Noise in the hall.*)

Please let me finish. The commission should check the activity of the investigatory team itself only after the verification, which will be absolutely correct legally, of the accusation made by Comrades Gdlyan and Ivanov and depending on the results of such a verification. To this end the commission should be vested, like any parliamentary investigation commission, with the broadest authority and the right to summon any official to provide necessary explanations. I now propose from this point of view limiting ourselves to the discussion of the proposed list of the commission's members. Let us discuss whatever particular objections there may be against individual people. If there are none, let us approve the commission's composition and enable it to begin its work.

Unfortunately, my proposal was not heeded. The leadership had no intention of investigating corruption of top party and government bodies. Nor did the Procurator's Office dare to start criminal proceedings against Gdlyan and Ivanov.

The First Congress declared that the press campaign must be halted. Accordingly, neither statements by the Procurator's Office nor accusations by Gdlyan and Ivanov against the Procurator's Office

were to be made while the commission was at work. But the truce was broken before long with each side loudly claiming that the other was at fault. The storm of mutual recriminations raged on.

This drama turned to farce. Gdlyan spoke (and people believed him) about certain documents that had been stowed away "for safety's sake" and said that the investigatory team had also collected compromising material against Gorbachev. Later, he contradicted himself, saying that Gorbachev was not involved and that such insinuations came from his enemies. The line of defense obviously was shifting with the political tides.

It is impossible to imagine a law-governed state in which there is no response to an ungrounded accusation of the country's leader's involvement in grave crimes. The president of a normal law-governed state would be obliged to start libel proceedings to defend his honor and dignity. We needed a special parliamentary commission to investigate accusations against our country's highest official and determine whether he should be held politically liable (which would entail, at the very least, his resignation). If his innocence were established, the commission would recommend appropriate legal action against his accusers. Its findings should be handed over to the Procurator's Office or other investigatory bodies.

Had this been done, the Gdlyan-Ivanov storm would have subsided rapidly. For some reason, Gorbachev muffed this chance to put a curb on irresponsible accusations. Gdlyan, growing bolder, predicted that Gorbachev's regime would be overthrown and named the very day—it would be during the May Day demonstration on Red Square, he said. Something bizarre was going on.

The 1990 May Day events turned out to be a miserable parody of the East European revolutions of autumn 1989. Insulting slogans and shouts from a group of radical democrats prompted Gorbachev and the rest of the members of the government to make a hasty exit from the rostrum on the mausoleum. Gdlyan and Ivanov proved to be single-issue politicians who made no substantial contribution to the solution of other political problems. In any case, their sensational revelations were soon eclipsed by ones from a far more intriguing source—KGB Major-General Oleg Kalugin, who revealed the depths of KGB corruption.

The Gdlyan-Ivanov parliamentary commission, led not by a lawyer but a historian, offered a sobering lesson for our Tbilisi commission. Had we let ourselves get mixed up in interminable squabbles, we would never have gotten to the bottom of the matter.

When the time came for the Supreme Soviet to hear the commission's final conclusion, the hearing was postponed several times. Finally, it was scheduled for the third session of the summer 1989 Supreme Soviet. The hall was packed to the gills with members of the Supreme Soviet; people's deputies who were not members of the Supreme Soviet; the entire collegium of the Procurator's Office; many members of the Politburo and the government. And, of course, the press box was full.

Only deputies Gdlyan and Ivanov were absent.

Apparently fearing that their parliamentary immunity might be stripped and criminal proceedings instituted against them, with the specter of eventual arrest, the heroic investigators had prudently taken off for Armenia. Even their erstwhile admirers found this unnerving. Gdlyan and Ivanov clearly were not prepared to refute the accusations; the documents they'd had "stowed away for safety's sake" were a strategic ploy, or an outright bluff.

Deputies from Central Asian republics acted decisively. One after another, they declared the Moscow investigators guilty of "racism against the Uzbek people." The situation was escalating: accusations of legal violations had been replaced by political recriminations.

As the saying goes, curses, like chickens, come home to roost. Gdlyan and Ivanov were being victimized by the same kind of wild accusations they had hurled at others. Aware that political hysteria in parliament might have unpredictable consequences, I prepared carefully for the decisive session at which I defended the absent investigators.

In the end, the Supreme Soviet elected not to deprive deputies Gdlyan and Ivanov of their parliamentary immunity, censured the actions of the Procurator's Office itself, and agreed to have the opposing investigators dismissed. The Supreme Soviet judged the confrontation between the investigators and the Procurator's Office to have ended in a draw.

Gdlyan and Ivanov found themselves out of a job. True, they were offered work on the legislation committee of the Supreme Soviet, which would compensate at least materially for their loss of employment. But they chose another tack—they plunged into a new political campaign, and got themselves elected deputies in the Armenian parliament. This guaranteed them parliamentary immunity, had the Supreme Soviet changed its mind and left them at the mercy of the Procurator General.

Thus, our heroes were finally transformed from investigators into politicians (with an unofficial sideline as "detectives"). Their case petered out of its own accord, with the last flash of interest in it registered during the alleged "seizure" of Leningrad television by deputies of the Leningrad City Council in spring 1990.

It wasn't actually "seized;" a session of the city council merely decided to grant live airtime to People's Deputy Nikolai Ivanov. The TV authorities, still apparently convinced that the story about documents stashed away had some truth to it, quailed at the thought of having to answer to Moscow for any "scandal." The council delegation that accompanied Ivanov to the studio did not twist the authorities' arms and behaved quite peacefully, but the apocryphal tale of the television station's "seizure" was taken up eagerly by the mass media.

Ivanov spoke for several hours, showed film clips of his investigation, threatened the Moscow apparatchiks, and rehashed the stuff of old newspaper clippings. No one stopped him from talking on and on. In the morning, the city was cranky from lack of sleep and disillusionment. The idol of yesterday had shot himself in the foot.

Was it a political draw?

Yes—except that Gdlyan and Ivanov left behind an IOU that was paid out of the electors' pockets. I don't mean the hours of TV time, although they did cost money; I'm speaking about the decline of interest in politics in a country which for many decades had had no politics. I mean the wave of civic apathy that followed such parliamentary draws.

Conclusions

As a lawyer who has trained many members of the law-enforcement agencies of our country, I have heard more than once from them that things haven't changed much since Gdlyan and Ivanov were at work. The system has legitimized violations of legal procedure, and the attendant degradation of the Soviet law-enforcement system remains firmly embedded.

This is not to say that the Procurator's Office and courts are manned by dishonest and mercenary people. On the contrary, the majority of their personnel are honest and decent people. But the system as a whole, the entire mechanism of law enforcement agencies operating as a repressive appendage of the party machine of ideological suppression, has led to perversion of the law and erosion of human rights for all—the accused, the investigators, and the judges themselves.

The Uzbek "cotton case" could have been described as the crime of the century had the likes of it not been going on in every part of the country and every sphere of our national economy.

This is one of the reasons why we, potentially one of the world's richest countries, have slipped into poverty and are on the verge of economic ruin.

Has much changed?

Where are deputies' demands to set up a parliamentary commission to investigate the activity of the ANT corporation? The government and the Procurator's Office assured everybody that they would investigate. After that—silence.

And what about the conclusions of our Tbilisi commission? The Congress of People's Deputies voted to accept our recommendations. Were they implemented? No. No one has been brought to justice, although the commission's report listed the names of those whom it deemed criminally liable for the April 9 tragedy. Even the simplest decision by the Second Congress on the television screening of a film shot by KGB cameramen in front of Government House on that horrible, bloody night was shelved as if there had been no decision— nor any massacre, for that matter.

It seems clear that the strength and energy of the reformers who launched perestroika in 1985 were insufficient to destroy the criminal social system which could extinguish any impulse or attempt to reform it.

Yes, the "revolution from above" gave the country glasnost, then virtual freedom of speech, the elimination of the party's monopoly, and much more. Our foreign policy became more civilized. Gorbachev and his disciples managed to help the peoples of Eastern Europe liberate themselves from totalitarian socialism and grow the first seedlings of parliamentarianism in their own countries.

But the transition to a market system has become a line beyond which the system cannot retreat, a last ditch in which it is prepared to die. For more than five years, the country has been exhausting itself, fighting the agonizing totalitarian system of "socialism with an inhuman face." For more than five years we have lived in struggle and expectation. Those of us who urged the resignation of the Procurator General won a mini-victory of sorts. Sukharov did resign, following Ligachev, Chebrikov, and the others into political oblivion. Is that any reason to rejoice?

We know today that political corpses can be self-rejuvenating. A dying dragon may poison and destroy everything around it with its deaththroes.

7

"Deputy Sakharov's Amendment"

Hope, in the pits that darkly yawn . . .

Alexander Pushkin

The focal point of 1989 was the campaign for the repeal or amendment of Article 6 of the Union Constitution, which legally enshrined the leading role of the Communist Party in Soviet life. The question of abolishing the ideological and political monopoly of the party first came up during the elections of people's deputies. By spring 1989, many candidates were already calling for a change to a multi-party system.

The demand for repeal of Article 6 was part of my own platform, and I soon found myself at war with the party apparat. The battle was waged right up to election day with time-tested methods: anonymous pamphlets attacking me, churned out by district party committees; rowdies interfering with my meetings with voters. But there was never any mention of Article 6. They tried instead to discredit me personally, criticizing other parts of my program, but scrupulously avoiding the merest hint that Article 6 might be at issue.

When it became clear that virtually all the Leningrad party functionaries had failed to catch the election wave and instead had drowned in the sea of public discontent, the April plenary session of the Leningrad regional party committee "questioned the color of the membership cards" of those communists who were calling for an end to the party's "leading role."

To be honest, I had no premonition that Article 6 would figure so prominently at the First Congress of People's Deputies. I could see that our efforts would have to be concentrated on the formation of new organs of power, drafting an official decree on power, and institutionalizing the Congress and the Supreme Soviet as the new supreme bodies of state authority. This meant giving priority to the campaign for the transfer of all power to the soviets (councils), not to the fight against Article 6. Of course, these two questions were related, but the first step towards the transfer of political power could have been made without abolishing the party's ideological monopoly. This corresponded fully to the declaration of the 19th Party Conference on the division of functions between state and party bodies, and it appeared genuinely feasible at this time.

The 19th Party Conference had stopped at half measures, to be sure; state bodies were to govern the country, while party bodies were to produce ideology. . . . So long as Article 6 remained in force, this division would be largely fictive. But the formula freed us to concentrate our efforts on the technical issues of setting up new government bodies. We could afford a little patience.

The deputies made every effort to prevent the old nomenklatura system of selection from infiltrating the new institutions. We succeeded in part, but at what a price! The very fact that we were not completely successful proved the correctness of our assessment of our own strength vis-à-vis the party apparat. We pointed the parliamentary battle in precisely this direction, starting with the essential aim of restricting the nomenklatura's omnipotence. It would have been political adventurism or naiveté to hope for anything more at the First Congress.

But the question of the repeal of Article 6 came up even before the Congress sessions began, when Andrei Sakharov raised it at the preliminary meeting of deputies with the party leadership.

I think Sakharov himself was well aware that what he said always led to things being done later on. The repeal of Article 6 had to be raised immediately; when it would actually come about was another matter entirely. This strategy underlay all of Sakharov's proposals. It was his style. Sakharov would say things that seemed untimely to his contemporaries; which is why his ideas never became dated the following day.

Sakharov found support from the deputies who would later form the Inter-Regional Group. Yuri Afansyev, the rector of the Moscow Historical-Archival Institute, spoke particularly forcefully in Sakharov's favor. Still, the theme of Article 6 and the abolition of the leading role of the Communist Party was sounded only sporadically at the Congress, for the reason that the deputies and the public at large were not psychologically and politically prepared for a full consideration of this issue. I knew of people far removed from the communist position on this who, in summer 1989, were certain that repeal of Article 6 would lead to bloody chaos and civil war. Others simply viewed the party's leading role as a given. The idea had been drummed into our heads for so long that removing it from social consciousness required time. The deputies generally adhered to the stand approved at the Party Conference: it was wrong for the party to meddle in economic matters or questions connected with the creation of councils. For the time being, only a few were willing to venture further, and even they mentioned Article 6 only in passing. Sakharov received only nominal support. He remained the democratic leader of the Congress and of our people, a matchless and idealistic leader marching alone, far in the vanguard.

I can confirm firsthand that the amendment proposed by Sakharov was not discussed even off the record. In other words, both Sakharov's opponents and his supporters denied the urgency of the issue.

At the First Congress, I myself mentioned repeal of Article 6 only in the course of seconding Deputy Obolensky's bid to run against Gorbachev for chairman of the Supreme Soviet. I argued that Obolensky was not a member of the party, and that the Constitution should stipulate that all posts in the state apparat be open to nonmembers. I tried to make a case for specific legal sanction for those other than communists to occupy government posts up to, and including, chairman of the country's supreme legislative body. This, of course, meant amending Article 6. But I decided for strategic reasons to let this remain tacit. To do otherwise would have been a waste of breath. I confined my words to support for "equal political rights for non-party and party members," a notion more palatable to the audience. True, in the light of democratic principles of the functioning of state power, my proposal looked rather inane; how could a country "ruled by the people" talk about establishing equality between the majority and a minority comprising Communist Party members? The absence of such equality was evidence that democratization wasn't yet underway. In such a situation, only restoration of the majority's right to exercise state power could put matters in order.

All the deputies, including Obolensky, knew full well that Gorbachev would be elected. At issue, however, was the principle of democratic elections. More than 800 deputies voted to include Obolensky's name on the list of candidates. This still fell short of the number required to put him on the ballots, and Gorbachev was elected unopposed. A year later, however, there would be a full slate of candidates running for president of the USSR and chairman of the Supreme Soviet.

Herein lay the seeds of the Inter-Regional Group of Deputies, as Gavril Popov and Yuri Afansyev reacted to this vote by proposing that the radical democrats in Parliament organize themselves. It was a sobering lesson in the dynamics of power: had Gorbachev supported the idea of contested elections and used his authority to get Obolensky's name on the ballot, it would have been much tougher putting together this interregional opposition.

Real support for the idea floated by Andrei Sakharov at the First Congress came from the press rather than from the deputies. The newspapers of 1989 give a clear picture of how public opinion matured gradually toward acceptance of this simple democratic idea. Sporadic statements by the radical fringe of journalists and political scientists in the most outspoken dailies and weeklies were followed by miners' demands for amendment or repeal of Article 6. . . . The crucial event was the founding of the Inter-Regional Group. Its co-chairman Sakharov made certain that its platform included a clearcut demand for the demonopolization of power and repeal of Article 6.

The issue snowballed. At every session of the Supreme Soviet, someone would bring it up. The powers-that-be could ignore it no longer.

Article 6 precipitated a stormy debate at the Second Congress which opened December 12, 1989. The democratic forces were fresh from victory at the second session of the Supreme Soviet, where the Inter-Regional Group had proposed that the question of a change in the Constitution and repeal of Article 6 be put on the agenda of the forthcoming Second Congress. There was heated debate. Sakharov took part, although he was not a member of the Supreme Soviet. I spoke in support of Sakharov, concentrating on technical legal grounds for repeal (Article 6 contradicted Articles 1 and 2 of the Constitution, which proclaim the "rule of the people").

The vote in the Supreme Soviet was close. We fell only three votes short of getting the question onto the agenda. It was clear it would come up one way or another, and both sides could see that the next time, the democrats would carry the day.

The Second Congress of People's Deputies

The Inter-Regional Group decided to make every effort to get the question onto the Congress agenda. A motion to this effect was made on the first day, and we were confident we would prevail. But we underestimated the thoroughness of the apparat's preparations. The Second Congress proved far more complacent than the First, far more tentative about independent judgements and decisions.

We lost badly: some 60 percent of the deputies chose not to support us.

Article 6 of the Constitution cut off the emergence of political pluralism at its very roots. It left room only for "socialist pluralism," the oxymoronic concept Ligachev had tried so hard to cultivate. Without a multiparty system there would be no parliamentary clash of views and hence no developed consensus. Absent such a system, there could be only a "socialist parliament," a variant of the tsarist boyars council. "The Tsar dictates and the boyars say *so be it.*"

The people's deputies still regarded Article 6 as the national ethic rather than the will of the political leadership. Communist ideology did not become a state religion overnight. It has long been the catechism of every citizen involved in the power structure.

The advocates of Article 6 asked: Did it exist under Stalin? No. The article institutionalizing the leading role of the Communist Party first appeared in the 1977 Brezhnev Constitution. But the party was already at the helm long before Article 6, so the article was not to blame for violations of law.

Brezhnev's Constitution merely gave formal constitutional status to what had been taking shape since the 1920s, and what by the Stalinist era was the Party's *de facto* ideological imperative. The explicit statement of the vanguard role of the party introduced under Brezhnev gave legal justification for the powerlessness of the already long-impotent soviets [councils]. The impetus was a reaction to Khrushchev's "thaw," and the result was the active revival of Stalinism, the renaissance of totalitarianism.

Some said the party was the only political force capable of uniting our "best and brightest." In a situation of great flux, no restrictions should be placed on our only support and hope for renewal. The party had initiated perestroika; they argued that we should be grateful for the "new thinking" and efforts to modernize the political system. Repeal of Article 6 would lead to the country's disintegration . . .

Ironically there was some truth to these arguments. By taking upon itself the functions of state power, the party had become the structural support for this power. Repeal would mean a shift in the political system's center of gravity and transfer of real power from the party to the state.

The consequences would be unpredictable. Reforms don't set off social explosions, though—*delays* in reform do that. It was impossible to build a law-governed state so long as Article 6 was in place. Failure to repeal it sooner or later would end in "revolution from below." A choice had to be made.

Credit must be given Gorbachev for launching political reform precisely by advancing the idea of a law-governed state. Neither party ideologues on the lookout for heresy nor liberal-minded jurists seemed to realize that a *law-governed state* not only required observance of justice and human rights, it represented a knife in the very heart of the system.

Apart from a few politicians in Gorbachev's entourage, only one man had grasped and appreciated everything clearly from the very beginning and this was Sakharov. He was not a jurist, but he saw that this idea was a helping hand stretched directly to him.

The events that ensued may seem somewhat strange and illogical to the uninitiated. Barely two months after the end of the Congress, the February 1990 plenary meeting of the Central Committee voted almost unanimously to repeal Article 6, and the party renounced its monopoly on power, clearing the way for a multi-party system.

It could be said that in February 1990, the Communist Party reconstituted itself in the USSR as a *political* party, not just a part of the state structure, an ideologized substitute for a genuine state. And rank-and-file party members were faced squarely with the question: Who are we, utopian fanatics, or people drawn into the ranks of an alien party by historical and political factors?

What happened? Why did everything change so drastically in just two months?

In retrospect, it seems less surprising, even inevitable. Article 6 had actually become a threat to the system's viability. Even conservatives could see that it had to go, the sooner the better.

East Europe's communist regimes had fallen. On February 4, on the eve of the plenary meeting, a half-million-strong demonstration following the Eastern Europe lead, poured down the streets of Moscow to a rally that lasted for several hours on Manège Square. A platform was set up on a flatbed just below the windows of the Moskva Hotel, where provincial members of the Central Committee were staying. The demonstrators dubbed it the "February revolution." And it was.

On the eve of the demonstration, its organizers were received by Gorbachev's aide, Anatoly Lukyanov, who gave permission for them to rally not only in front of the Moscow City Council, but also under the windows of the Moskva Hotel. The militia were ordered to escort the column and help the demonstration's organizers.

This time, the leaders of the state evinced realism and political intuition. If only this were always so. By February 1990, popular fronts and other informal organizations had shown had the people felt about the omnipotence of party structures. The tension was so thick, even the conservatives could not ignore it. Practically all the conservative speakers at the plenary session devoted time to criticism of Gorbachev's proposal to repeal Article 6 and condemnation of the "so-called democrats," the "informals," with their newfangled pluralism and other "innovations." They decried the "discrediting of the party and socialism." And yet, with the same near-unanimity, they voted yes to the party's abdication of its monopoly on power. Was this just reflexive obedience to the leader? I still have not figured out how Gorbachev, in what may have been a key victory for him, managed to get the Central Committee in line.

But the victory came terribly late.

Article 6 was obviously going to be the central issue at the March 1990 Third Congress of People's Deputies. Far from all the deputies were ready to bow to the inevitable, however. Party functionaries again raised the specter of the party's loss of authority, the weakening of power, the threat of chaos. Again, there was talk of the "consolidation of all healthy forces round the party." But it sounded like the plaints of an incorrigible Don Juan after divorce had stripped him of his family and property. A compromise formula was proposed: "The Communist Party and other parties and political organizations have the right to conduct political activity . . ." Someone remarked that it was like including in the Constitution: "Yegor Kuzmieh Ligachev and other Soviet citizens have the right to work, rest and leisure, etc." The audience burst out laughing, and that was the end of that. An overwhelming majority—more than two-thirds!—of the deputies voted to "divorce" Article 6. There was a standing ovation when the results of the vote were announced.

Instead of the prophesied chaos, we saw democratization accelerate. Work was stepped up on the draft law on parties and public organizations, and the law on the freedom of the press. The climate at the Congress changed; it was as though a time bomb had been defused.

The President

As a sober-minded politician, Gorbachev realized that if he failed to convince the conservatives to repeal Article 6, he'd stand little chance of becoming president. Democratic forces were bound to unite against a presidential candidate who still represented the "party of the vanguard."

During the discussion of Gorbachev's candidacy, I took the floor and argued that Article 6 had been repealed, the party had ceased to play the role of a monopolist usurping state and political power. Of course, this was all to the good. But—I added—the country must have a vertical structure of authority, the core that holds together any civilized state. Historical experience shows us that presidential rule can become such a core. Indeed, there is no other way of protecting the administration of the country from party dictates.

"Deputy Sakharov's Amendment"

I no longer recall who, during the Third Congress, dubbed the repeal of Article 6 "Deputy Sakharov's Amendment." Andrei Sakharov had launched the struggle for the abolition of the party's monopoly on power back at the First Congress. And it became what was perhaps his greatest victory.

It was a victory won at the cost of his own life. He died on December 14, 1989.

Sakharov did not live to see the Armenian pogroms in Baku, nor the butchery the system unleashed when troops were called into the capital of Azerbaijan, nor Moscow's "February Revolution."

Article 6 collapsed in March 1990, but at the Inaugural Congress of the Russian Communist Party in June 1990, and at the 28th Party Congress that July, many delegates chose to talk on as if nothing had happened. (Bad habits are hard to break.)

The issue of depoliticizing the system's punitive organs—the army, the KGB, the Ministry of the Interior—remained unresolved. The state security service was almost 100 percent communist, and communists remained in the majority in the army and militia. At Supreme Soviet sessions, I had pointed out that this was contrary to our present constitution, a *de facto* continuation of something that had been abolished *de jure*. To the credit of the people's deputies, they proposed including in the Constitution a line about the depoliticization of the army and the police, including the secret police. Sakharov, too, spoke of this on several occasions, and although he was not heeded at the time, the process later got underway. During the summer of 1990, many members of the militia, the judicial system, and the procuracy responded to calls by republic and local sessions of people's deputies by quitting the party. And this process had begun in state security bodies as well.

I would rank the repeal of Article 6 as the most radical event in our country's life since October 1917. History has consigned to the archives the anti-human and anti-popular regime of one-party rule established by the Bolsheviks. Its reign and its death throes were stained with blood; its actual fall was bloodless. But only after the punitive organs have been depoliticized thoroughly will we be able to say over Sakharov's grave: *Andrei Dmitrievich, your life's cause has triumphed.*

The draft Constitution of the Union of Soviet Republics of Europe and Asia drawn up by Andrei Sakharov is his spiritual testament. Strictly speaking, this document cannot be called a draft constitutional *law:* it does not have the precise juridical wording required by a constitution and does not reflect many questions that must be included in the text of any constitution. But it contains ideas of global importance for building a common European and world home, and which deserve careful study by politicians and jurists.

Article 2 of Sakharov's draft constitution proclaims the aim of the people and the state to be "a happy and meaningful life, material and spiritual freedom, welfare, peace and security for the citizens of the country, and for all people on Earth regardless of their race, nationality, sex, age and social status."

We shall not find such a provision in any constitution anywhere now in force. All constitutions define citizens' rights and freedoms, welfare, etc., but none of them includes clauses dealing with a happy and spiritually full life as the true aim of each human society, each human being. And is there any other more lofty aim?

The abundance of material values cannot by itself make people happy. It is only an indispensable condition, a foundation on which it is possible to build a flourishing society in which man has a life full of meaning and happiness.

Another idea of Sakharov's which, in my view, must be reflected in all constitutions, is the idea of the priority of "the global ideas of the survival of mankind over any regional, state, national, class, party, group and personal interest" (Article 3).

This provision is not part of any of today's constitutions, for the idea of sovereignty still prevails. But Sakharov was able to look into the future and realize that, if only for ecological reasons, humanity would not continue to survive if priority were not give to global and general human objectives. You don't have to be a prophet to guess that the time is not far off when such a provision will appear as a central principle of constitutional legislation.

Related to this is another idea promulgated by Sakharov—the idea of the convergence of the socialist and the capitalist systems that alone could ensure the cardinal solution of global and internal problems of mankind.

The idea of convergence, put forward at the end of the 1970s by John Kenneth Galbraith and other Western thinkers, was adapted by Sakharov with reference to our society. At one time, this was used as grounds for accusations that Sakharov had betrayed his homeland. But time has passed, and our consciousness has now reached the stage of accepting this idea as a route toward a united Europe, and a united mankind.

Mention should also be made of Article 13's provision, that "the Union does not have the objectives that include expansion, aggression and Messianism." The history of the twentieth century has given us all too many examples of aggressive ignorance and vulgar belief in the ability to "bestow" happiness on mankind (whether or not it wants it), that led to tragedy for entire nations.

Communist Messianism, for all its promises that our people would live to see "true communism," in their land, and its claims that it alone had the key to progress for mankind, brought only degradation, moral and material, to our people—and to other peoples as well.

A new social contract must renounce Messianism, expansion, and aggression for the sake not only of ourselves, but for other peoples seeking some reason to trust in a revived Russia.

Sakharov may not have been a jurist, but in his draft for a new constitution he proposed many political decisions which came to pass (for instance, reduction of the number of central ministries, accompanied by a fundamental revision of the functions of the central government). Some are yet to be realized (different conditions for the entry of different republics into a new Union, the toleration of two or more languages in republics, along with Russian as an official language, etc.).

Sakharov's constitutional ideas must be taken into account during the forthcoming overhaul of our politics and the creation of a true civil society among our people.

The time for his ideas has come.

8

The First Little Putsch
Leningrad, 1989

Well, and there will be an upheaval! There's going to be such
an upset as the world has never seen before . . . Russia will be
overwhelmed with darkness, the earth will weep for its old
gods . . .
Well, then we shall bring forward . . . whom?

Fyodor Dostoyevsky

The apparat did not take the democrats seriously until the Second
Congress in winter 1989. By then things were completely different.

Back during the First Congress, a Politburo member could stand
in the corridor and comment loudly, "Look at that riff-raff!"

And it was a motley crew holding forth about God knows what.
Their voices could be heard going on from the rostrum and in the
aisles . . . Impatient with their own leaders, they were getting out of
hand, seizing the mikes almost by force. But it took a while before
they began to pose a threat to the system itself.

Eventually, however, the democratic threat started to get serious. The apparat's alarms went off when the "riff-raff" wrested control
of legislative power, and the drafting of laws moved from the peace
and quiet of bureaucrats' offices to the noisy sessions of parliamentary
committees and commissions.

We came up short at the First Congress, but at the session of the Supreme Soviet following the formation of perhaps the most democratic of all the committees, that on legislation, power started to tilt towards the "riff-raff." Why that particular committee? Because it brought together professionals, people who had known each other for decades and who treated one another with respect.

At the first session of the Supreme Soviet, the apparat tried to take us on. When the draft law on the press, which the apparat had tried fervently to delay, was at last completed, they had the gall to pull a switch, substituting a different draft.

We were already being taken seriously—they were wheeling out the heavy artillery.

Late in autumn 1989, a rally was held in a swank Moscow hall in honor of my favorite newspaper, *Moscow News*. Somehow, the event left a bitter taste in my mouth. Everything was lovely. The occasion brought together the cream of the intelligentsia, prominent actors, journalists, and writers. But I was pained and embarrassed to see and hear what came from the stage.

The target selected for "roasting" was our country's political leader, who had just begun democratic changes. Some of the wit was well-aimed, but its form went beyond the bounds of decency. Had people already forgotten what it was like to listen to radio jamming at night, to breathe stale air without hope?

It seemed we were not yet ready to face the truth about the kind of country we lived in, what kind of people it had made of us. First and foremost, Gorbachev's perestroika made the Soviet people take a good hard look at themselves. And what was happening to us then made it painfully clear how unfree and uncivilized we were. We had a chance to take civic action—but we were not ready.

The conservative forces were taking advantage and closing ranks. "Back to the dictatorship of the proletariat!" "We won't allow perestroika to strike a blow at communism!" It was the creeping coup d'état of the counterrevolutionary apparat, who had decided that the time was ripe to put an end to the specter of democracy and parliamentarianism. The first offensive was staged in Leningrad in the fall of 1989, and it shook the city and the nation.

Parliamentary Autumn

The first parliamentary autumn was setting in. I spent nearly all my time in Moscow, working with the committee on legislation and attending the session of the Supreme Soviet, returning to Leningrad only on weekends. More loudly and more often, talk was heard that the Leningrad regional committee had not changed its stripes under its new leader, Boris Gidaspov, the former Director-General of the State Institute of Applied Chemistry, who had come out of nowhere to be hand-picked for the job by the previous first party secretary, the undistinguished Yuki Solovyov. Informal organizations were still being hounded. Nor had the city's executive committee or major industrial and managerial structures changed their methods.

To me, that meant that the system of power was headed for a fresh defeat in the spring 1990 elections of the Russian Congress of People's Deputies and the Leningrad city council. Democratic forces stood to enjoy an even more impressive victory than in spring 1989.

The city authorities had some premonitions of this. As a deputy dealing with leading district and city officials, I saw fear and confusion in their eyes. It made their reactions unpredictable. The chairman of a district executive committee would say to a voter, "Let your Sobchak solve your problem!" A week later, the same official would phone me to ask if he could do anything for me, if I had any questions for him?

Both boorishness and obsequiousness were evidence of panic among the officials.

Something had to give.

Gidaspov's November 22 rally came like a bolt from the blue.

Background

In the November 7, 1989 parade, commemorating the Bolshevik revolution, the Leningrad Popular Front had its own column. An entire street was filled with a 30,000-strong procession of democratic forces. Members of Memorial [the group dedicated to memorializing the victims of Stalinism] and the Voters' Association marched along with the Popular Front. The civil parade was led by people's deputies.

Perhaps that was why the authorities decided to strike from the rear: when the lead marchers passed the viewing stand where party chief Boris Gidaspov stood smiling, the militia cut off the tail of the column. Some 100 to 150 people lost their banners and posters and were shoved along to Nevsky Prospekt. They showed restraint; nobody started a fight. They were held there for some twenty minutes; then, the cordon parted. It remains a mystery who issued the order, but the meaning of the provocation was apparent.

The Leningrad party ideological chief told a reporter from the newspaper *Vecherny Leningrad* (Leningrad Evening News): "If you want to know whether there were some incidents during the parade, I can tell you that there were none." Soon enough, even the participants probably forgot what had occurred.

On November 10, the infamous reactionary, Nina Andreyeva, appeared on television for the first time. She had agreed to give an interview to the program "Vzglyad" [Outlook]. The interview turned into a monologue, as Nina Andreyeva went on and on about "shadow economy" businessmen who were infiltrating the political scene and striving to destroy socialism.

On that same day, *Vecherny Leningrad* reported that a plenary session of the Vasileostrovsky district party committee had demanded the convening of "an emergency Party congress." The "spontaneous" demand must have been prepared well in advance, for when the idea of an emergency congress was proposed (by a man of strong democratic views), a written resolution appeared as if by magic. It only goes to show that the conservatives knew how to exploit the initiative of some democrats to suit their own ends.

On November 13, in the pouring rain, the Vasileostrovsky district party committee staged a rehearsal of a "meeting putsch," a small, district-size "communist" rally. It was called "a meeting of Party activists." The speakers held forth from the balcony of the Kirov Palace of Culture, and their speeches differed little from Nina Andreyeva's reactionary monologue.

A Plan for a Coup D'État

Evidently, the organizers felt that the experiment was a success. On November 15, *Leningradskaya Pravda* carried a "manifesto" by the secretary of the regional party committee in the "Standpoint" section [i.e., its op-ed page—*ed*] under the title, "Who benefits from the crisis?," the author echoing Nina Andreyeva's words: ". . . the 'shadow economy' businessmen, who already have about 500 billion rubles in their hands, and their arrival on an open political arena . . . They already have quite a few defenders among journalists, scientists, and lawmakers. But this is just the beginning."

He went on to decry "the thoughtless and hasty reappraisal of historical facts and values," "the destruction of the image of a homeland, and the abandonment of ideals achieved by such enormous effort." He prescribed a remedy for the crisis: "The introduction of martial law." This was not a panacea, the author observed, but "a means facilitating reforms and making it possible to overcome the crisis."

Since martial law did not guarantee a political victory, he suggested giving local party organizations the right to recall any communist deputy registered with them "to assert a genuine pluralism of views and glasnost."

In other words, the author was thinking in terms of a mechanism for crushing the deputies, more than eighty percent of whom were communists, as a political force.

What is most regrettable is that few people in the city, let alone the country as a whole, paid attention to that article, *which actually outlined a scheme for a coup d'état.*

On November 21, the Leningrad regional and city party committees began a joint plenary session. The city party leader was dismissed from his post, and Boris Gidaspov took over that position, in addition to the regional leadership.

The very title of Gidaspov's official report had the ring of a challenge: *To Safeguard the Socialist Ideals of Perestroika.* Here are some lines from it:

> We cease to be ourselves if we forego our socialist values and allow the fanatical pseudo-democrats to fool the people with their honey-sweet fairy tales of "people's capitalism," limitless democracy, and non-party glasnost . . .
>
> A pseudo-democratic truncheon comes down on all those who dare to express a dissenting view, and the idea that our society is incurable is being whipped up . . .
>
> The people's minds are being befuddled by the images of ubiquitous bureaucrats, apparatchiks, chauvinists, Stalinists, and anti-Semites . . .

The Leningrad Popular Front was accused of having a secret plan to dismantle socialism and make society capitalist.

Liberal-minded deputies found themselves barred from speaking and driven from the rostrum. Gidaspov's supporters had more success. And throughout, believe it or not, the country had no idea what was going on.

The city "communist" meeting took place on November 22. What had been schemed in the quiet of the Smolny offices during the preceding weeks and rehearsed in the Vasileostrovsky District now poured out into public squares.

Gidaspov himself conducted the meeting.

The Leningrad functionaries had understood earlier than others that tomorrow they might find themselves on the scrap heap of history. They were the first to launch a campaign against Gorbachev's policy. Although they were cautious enough not to come out with an open challenge and call for the restoration of Stalinism, only a child could have failed to realize what the full-time defenders of the system had in mind.

Thank God we had impartial television in those days. The broadcast of the "meeting putsch" was enough to awaken the country at that fatal hour.

I was in Moscow at the time and watched only part of the November 22 meeting. I was horrified by the bitterness and atmosphere of collective hatred.

It reminded me of newsreels of the 1930s, when fanatic crowds demanded death to "the Trotskyite-Zinovyevite fosterlings." I admit I was scared. How mired we still were in the past! How strongly Stalinism was entrenched in us. Among those speaking were writers and engineers, though most of the speakers, of course, were apparatchiks. But they were all educated people from whom one might have expected some attempt at logic. But no, there were only political exhortations, only the frenzy of Stalinism, the call for an "iron fist" that would put things in order. And it was all the more horrifying that the speakers were a long way from the top echelons of the nomenklatura. You'd think that the secretary of a factory party committee would be aware of the problems confronting the "ordinary folks" around him—but then he would open his mouth and out would come words no normal person would ever utter.

I was scheduled to appear the next day on the TV program "The Fifth Wheel." The previously prepared program was scrapped to deal with Gidaspov's meeting.

I returned to find Leningrad a changed city. It was as if there had been no democratic victory in the spring. The meeting was the sole topic of conversation. Everyone anticipated worse to come.

I had no choice but to address Gidaspov directly from the TV screen. I said that if he believed he could run the city like a munitions factory, he was grossly mistaken. Because, no matter what things had been done to Leningrad over the past seventy years, the city still remained a center of world culture and science. And, perhaps, the country's spiritual center. His proposed manner of governing was, for us, quite simply impossible. Decisions on our city's affairs had to be referred to its citizens. It was impermissible to conduct experiments without taking their view into account. I also had some rather harsh things to say about the November 22 meeting.

I spoke for about an hour and a half, a long time for TV.

Together with the chief correspondent of "The Fifth Wheel," Bella Kurkova, I left the television center after midnight. Neither of us had an official car, so we intended to say goodbye to each other and head home. We were nearing a trolley stop when a very dashing and impressive-looking young man approached us. He appeared so suddenly that I stiffened and, I guess, glared threateningly at him.

He didn't notice how tense I was.

"I'm an ex-paratrooper," he said. "I've finished my active service, and I live near here. My father is an officer, and he sent me to meet you. We watched the program, and Father told me to protect you because those SOB's could do anything to you now. I have a car, so I can take you home."

I want to thank this young man and his father. As we talked, we discovered that the TV staff had a van for us, after all, and three minutes later, I was at the entrance to my subway station.

I did not yet know that the whole city had watched the program, and that it would act like a fuse inserted into a grenade. The city had come out of its daze and was preparing protest actions against the onslaught of the communist orthodox. The Leningrad Popular Front asked for permission to hold a mass rally at the Sports and Concert Complex.

The anti-Gidaspov rally took place on December 6. I was back in Moscow, but I watched it on TV from beginning to end. From the very first minutes it was clear that the scheme devised by the Leningrad apparatchiks had flopped and was buried for good. Boris Gidaspov himself showed up and got hold of a mike. It was a pathetic performance.

Gidaspov tried to look confident, waving his clenched fist in the prewar communist salute—but it was a surrender. I saw the crowd in that square chanting "Resign! Resign!," I saw the emcee try to stop the chanting by waving "enough" behind Gidaspov's back, and I felt nothing but pity and shame for the out-of-place boss.

I do not think of myself as a swashbuckler by nature. I simply decided one day that to preserve my self-respect I must behave in a certain way and communicate on equal terms with any person, no matter what post he might hold or whatever he might do, and say only what I meant.

Perhaps I worked that out for myself for the first time at a meeting among deputies, party members, and members of the Politburo, which took place shortly before the Congress. I decided that I would speak only the truth and only on an equal footing. At first, I had to build up this very simple and natural pattern of behavior. Later on, it came naturally to me. I realized after that anyone who went in for compromises was creating additional difficulties for himself. Even if your behavior contradicted what was commonly accepted, it was better than trying to maneuver while looking over your shoulder. After a little while, those around you would get used to it, and your attitude would be accepted as quite natural.

I know I would have achieved nothing as a people's deputy had I not learned this truth: speak with the authorities as you would with your university colleagues or neighbors; and with "common people" as you would with the authorities—but without trying to ingratiate yourself with either.

During the Congress I often saw perplexity in the eyes of high-ranking officials: why is this man from God knows where talking to us like that? Whose protection has he got? More than once, I heard people say something like this: Sobchak has it good, he coordinates his statements with Gorbachev.

Well, I myself had thought for a long time that Yeltsin was one of Gorbachev's closest friends, and everything that happened to the former was to some extent a put-up job. Gorbachev had simply sacrificed Yeltsin for a while for tactical considerations. Until I got acquainted with both and saw the real correlation of forces, prejudices, and passions, I had been sure that I understood the "game."

The legend about Gorbachev's patronage was applied to me as well. It's true that before I had even opened my mouth publicly at the First Congress, Gorbachev knew my name. We had even traveled to China at the same time (of course it was not important that we were in different parts of that vast country!). And "perspicacious" viewers simply did not know that my surname was easily remembered because it is rather unusual, and also because I had spoken three times at meetings with Gorbachev before the Congress. That is how rumors, legends, and fabrications are born.

What happened to Boris Gidaspov? The press had already diagnosed Gidaspov's problem quite accurately: a case of the bends. Such a meteoric rise would be a strain on anyone. As the director of an institute, a defense contractor spoiled inside the military-industrial complex by funds and supplies always delivered on time, Gidaspov was used to absolute authority over his subordinates. He brought this style over into his new civilian job. The representative of the system won out over the scientist. Faced by the pluralistic freedom of the urban political scene, Gidaspov failed to master the new methods of activity at a time when political life was becoming increasingly democratic. Instead, he fell back on the old familiar methods to avoid political bankruptcy.

As a new political figure he could survive only by freeing himself from the old apparat. It would have been an arduous task to reform it, but he never even tried.

So Gidaspov became a pawn in the old guard's hands, a hostage to Leningrad neo-Stalinism. His masters demanded decisive action against the renegade democrats. The apparat feared a second, and lethal, defeat in local and republican government elections. Only Gorbachev's resignation and the dissolution of the Soviet Parliament could avert disaster.

It was a dangerous game to play against the man who had actually appointed Gidaspov to his post. But yesterday's chemist had no other way out. The "meeting putsch," prepared thoroughly and not without ingenuity, was directed squarely against Gorbachev's policy. Gidaspov and those behind him wanted to accomplish in one go what Ligachev had failed to do over several years.

But Gidaspov overestimated his own strength and that of the party apparat. Nor did he get support from Moscow. (Although it is important to remember that the country's top conservative, Yegor Ligachev, was still in a position of power.)

"Back to the dictatorship of the proletariat!"
"We won't allow perestroika to strike a blow at communism!"
"Bring the Politburo to account!"
These were slogans from Gidaspov's meeting on November 22. And no matter what Boris Gidaspov himself might have said about "the extreme nature" of the slogans, everybody knew that they had not been written in private apartments, but printed at the city theatrical complex by order of the Regional Party Committee.

But the performance was a flop. The director should have quit. He stayed on, however; although he was forced to withdraw his candidacy for people's deputy. At the 28th Congress, Gidaspov even became a secretary of the Central Committee. In other words, despite his defeat in the autumn of 1989, his party career went on, at least on paper. In practice, Gidaspov's retreat from power was accepted fully by Leningrad's residents who voted for a democratic city council in spring of 1990.

Did Gidaspov, last of the omnipotent first secretaries of the Leningrad Regional Party Committee, agree?

I think not. But that's his own *personal* business.

9

The President of All Russia and of All the Outlying Provinces—Perhaps

The bureaucracy has the state . . . in its possession, as its private property.

Karl Marx

While the Coordinating Council of the Inter-Regional Group of Deputies held a meeting in the *Moskva* hotel in early December 1989, Andrei Sakharov, Yuri Chernichenko, and I stepped out into an adjacent room to argue about the abolition of Article 6 of the Constitution. Could it happen at the Second Congress? Would the Communist Party really give up its monopoly of power at the Congress? Without noticing, we went on to discuss the problem of the presidency.

Yuri Chernichenko said we would elect a president, and then allow ourselves to be hoodwinked. Even the Supreme Soviet could not actually control the activities of its chairman. It would be even more difficult to monitor the activities of a president.

Sakharov was more restrained.

"Evidently, we need a presidential form of government. But the President should be elected by the *entire* people. And he should be independent of the Central Committee and the Politburo . . ."

I agreed. But if we stalled over the presidency, I said, if we waited for national elections, we would lose time and enable the conservatives to gain strength. We might even be setting them up to win. At present, the head of state could rely only on the party, for other structures were either absent or too weak. He was dependent on the party apparat: the apparatchiks had elected him people's deputy, and that meant they could also recall him.

Chernichenko sighed.

"It may be not so bad to have a president—in principle. But we could also do without one."

Sakharov said nothing.

Later, I asked myself: why was Andrei Sakharov at first rather cool towards the idea of the presidency? Apparently, he was preoccupied at the time with an entirely different set of problems. He was busy writing his draft constitution, fighting Article 6 of the existing Brezhnev Constitution, trying to make rational sense of everything that was happening in what turned out to be the last weeks of his own life—including the downfall of the communist regimes in Europe and a nationwide warning strike already announced by the leaders of the left radicals.

All that occupied his mind much more than the subject of the presidency.

Several days before Sakharov's death, he and I returned to the subject.

Sakharov asked me what the presidency could actually give Gorbachev, who already had practically unlimited powers as General Secretary.

"You're right," I said, "but by using his powers as General Secretary he is strengthening precisely the authority of the Communist Party, including its power over the General Secretary himself. So this means that two ideas—the abolition of Article 6 and the introduction of the presidency—are closely linked." Only when Gorbachev received full *state* rather than *party* authority would he be able to abolish the party monopoly. Otherwise, he would simply lose power.

In a debate, Andrei Sakharov did not come over to your point of view right away. He would listen attentively to his opponent, and you could only guess from some barely visible signs whether what you said had become a subject for reflection, or whether he had rejected and forgotten it. And while during our first conversation on that subject I saw that the logic of my discourse had failed to convince him, and the talk, wandering off on a tangent, gave Sakharov no food for thought, during our second meeting, I became convinced that sooner or later Sakharov would support me on that issue. He did not yet agree with me, but he was meeting me halfway.

"Yes, it's worth thinking about," he said.

If I am not mistaken, those were the last words Andrei Sakharov said to me.

When did the idea of having a president in the USSR appear? Were we brought to it by the logic of democratic evolution, or did it devolve from crisis, the desire for security, the dream of order—or simply from the political fatigue of the people and their representatives?

The answer to this question is crucial to an analysis of political reform in our country.

Lawyers have discoursed at length on the shortcomings of the Soviet state structure. The soviets [councils] are collective bodies. Each deputy is accountable only for himself and only to his voters. There is no real mechanism for recalling a deputy, nor any party discipline. A deputy is not held responsible (how could he be, in such conditions?) for failing to carry out his campaign platform.

As a result, today's councils have as many political parties as they have deputies. Deputy blocs are ephemeral, and their actions often *ad hoc*. The average deputy is multi-incompetent and it is no wonder that the council sessions inevitably turn, at best, into coffee klatsches (at worst, they disrupt executive authority from *its* work).

These are congenital defects of the *system*. The councils are a pseudo-parliamentary (or, to be kind, "proto"-parliamentary) form of legislative power. Their weakness, amateurism, lack of democratic culture and legislative technique, made it possible for the party to usurp power—legislative, executive, and judicial—in the guise of "people's government." This is why the party found it so easy to turn itself into a parallel state replacing the bodies of government administration.

The last vestiges of *people's* soviets were eliminated in the late 1920s, when government bodies at all levels were first monitored; then duplicated by the party; and then replaced by the dictatorship of the party apparat.

Under party monopoly, the question of reforming the councils was moot. Why reform them? Deputies were appointed (their "elections" were a farce). The appointees met to endorse (always unanimously) decisions prepared for them in advance. Various official posts were linked to specific council seats. The head of Leningrad University was always a deputy to Russia's Supreme Soviet; the head of Moscow University was a member of the USSR Supreme Soviet. The Dean of the Leningrad University's Law Department was always a member of the Leningrad Soviet.

So long as the system remained immutable, there could be no talk of a presidency. The presidium of the USSR Supreme Soviet was a "collective president." Why hand supreme executive power to someone elected by all citizens?

When the country began to move from totalitarianism to democracy, with deputies truly elected by the population, and when such relatively democratic bodies of government as the parliamentary Supreme Soviets of the USSR and Russia came into being, it became clear that the chairman of the Supreme Soviet was not in any real sense the head of state.

In 1989, Gorbachev had no real rivals for this post. No one had any doubt that Gorbachev would be elected chairman. The inherent absurdity of his position soon became apparent as the country's leader was forced to sit all day listening to parliamentary debates, often about trivia. You were tempted to get up and ask: While the chairman of the Supreme Soviet is busy sorting out procedural points, who is running the country? Mikhail Sergeyevich, when do you have time to make decisions of national importance if you're sitting here with us in the Supreme Soviet from morning till night?

On the second day of the debate on the procedure of the Supreme Soviet sessions I could stand it no longer. I sent up a note to the chairman of the presidium. I apologized for taking the liberty of offering advice, but felt compelled to air my views.

Our junior orders have always mimicked their superiors' work style, so it was no surprise that the prime minister and members of the government and the Politburo also spent most of their working hours in the Supreme Soviet. If the head of state was sitting there what could be more important?

Gorbachev did not read my note aloud—but his appearances in the Supreme Soviet did become less frequent. Lukyanov started to chair most of the meetings. But there was still the question of what to do about the constitutional ambiguity of the chairman's position. Back in October 1989, when I had met with Gorbachev to discuss the work of the Tbilisi commission, I had told him that it was absolutely necessary to act on our findings or he would run the risk of a repetition of the bloody events of April 9. Gorbachev had lashed out: Why do you demand the impossible of me? Look at the Constitution—I'm no more than the speaker of parliament! I can't make the decisions you're talking about, I simply have no such powers!

That conversation left a deep impression on me. He had over-reacted the way someone does when you hit a nerve. Gorbachev, usually so approachable and moderate, suddenly flaring up like that! But he was right. If we went by the law (and not by the Soviet tradition whereby the General Secretary decided whatever he want-ed), the chairman of the Supreme Soviet was in many cases without real power.

I came to realize this only too well. After that I found myself in the same situation on the municipal level. Being chairman of the Leningrad city council gave me only the rights of a speaker and a representative. I had no real authority, yet responsibility by tradition rested with me.

At the Congresses of People's Deputies and at sessions of the Supreme Soviet, deputies made their complaints to Gorbachev about all the conflictual situations in the country. They were echoed by economic managers, speaking about interruptions in supplies, cul-tural workers complaining about the sorry plight of historic monu-ments, libraries, universities, and museums. Representatives of small ethnic groups also turned to Gorbachev, speaking to him with well-documented anguish about their nations' tragic fates under socialism.

Gorbachev could have acted as General Secretary, but that would have meant a return to Brezhnev's style. Besides, within the framework of the system, neither Brezhnev, nor Khrushchev, nor Stalin himself could have solved the problems engendered by its seventy years of power. This, despite the fact that in a state where the law is replaced by party resolutions, coercive and even tyrannical decisions were adopted and brought into life instantly. (Who of us can forget the stock formula of those years: "Guided by the valuable instructions of the General Secretary, the entire Soviet people"?)

The first steps towards democratization were so dramatic pre-cisely because the system could permit only a small step toward liberalizing the regime, and for a short time only. A totalitarian sys-tem leaves behind it a minefield built into both the country's social structure and the individual psychology of its citizens. And mines explode each time the system faces the danger of being dismantled and the country sees the prospect of genuine renewal.

During the first three years of perestroika, Gorbachev, acting within the framework of liberalization, could still make decisions as

General Secretary. The party apparat, though weakened, did exist, and this guaranteed that decisions would be carried out so long as they did not contravene the intrinsic substance of the system. But the liberalization of the regime and timid attempts to restructure it weakened party and government authority. A market mechanism was not launched in time, and the economic crisis deepened. And even the interethnic conflicts seemed to carry on the series of natural calamities and catastrophes triggered by Chernobyl.

The booby traps of totalitarianism went off one after another. The efforts to dismantle the system started by reformers from the Politburo had by then, more than once brought them to the brink of a political fiasco.

A series of attempts to solve interethnic conflicts evidently convinced Gorbachev that he lacked sufficient power to implement his decisions. Half the time, others would take the initiative and dump responsibility on him. And he had his own sins of omission and commission to answer for.

Matters reached a climax in Baku in January 1990 with the massacres of Armenians and the introduction of troops. Guilt for the tragedy in Tbilisi belonged squarely with the apparat, and Gorbachev did not take part in the fatal meeting chaired by Ligachev, but he did make the decision to send troops into Baku.

So discussions began on the need to strengthen executive power and on the possibility of instituting a presidency. Debate went on in the committees and commissions of the USSR Supreme Soviet. Two of Gorbachev's closest advisors, Yevgeni Primakov and Anatoli Lukyanov, were the first to bring it up. Their arguments were fair enough: it was necessary to relieve the head of state of having to waste time sitting in the Supreme Soviet. He had matters of national importance to attend to.

In January, the legislation committee's chairman joined me in putting out the first published discussion of the need for the presidency. The leaders of the Inter-Regional Group immediately voiced sharp criticism. Yuri Afanasyev objected that the presidency would strengthen party power and prestige and slow the collapse of the disintegrating "command" system.

Counter-arguments also appeared in the press: Stalin managed to grab power without being president, so the office itself was not crucial; presidential power would *replace* party power, so worrying about bolstering party prestige made no sense. The only way to go

from totalitarianism to democracy was via authoritarian power, was another view; otherwise, there would be chaos and total breakdown.

My own arguments?

1. Introduction of the presidency was necessary to separate legislative and executive power. That was the only way to make executive power adequately strong and independent.
2. A president was particularly needed in a country like ours. In a federative state (especially in view of attempts to create a confederation, as the Union republics raised their demand for sovereignty), it was vital that the head of state possess the most extensive powers compatible with democracy, and that was exactly what the presidency should be. The president would act as an arbitrator to settle disputes between republics. An arbitrator was also needed in the disputes between the republics and the center. Without that, it would be impossible to preserve an integral economic structure. Finally, a coordinator was needed in the economic, defense, and cultural sphere of relationships between the republics—to say nothing of the need to represent the country in international relations.

At first sight, the idea of a presidency fitted well the formula outlined by Gorbachev as early as the First Congress of People's Deputies: "A strong center—strong republics." But, as Andrei Sakharov observed, everything was turned upside down in this formula. It was necessary to begin with strong republics which would delegate some of their powers to the center. In that case, the center's strength would derive from the authority and confidence of the sovereign nations. As for the formula "A strong center—strong republics," it fits all too well the old concept that all power comes "from God and the Center." Gorbachev himself had not been free from such vestiges of imperial views as late as 1989.

The idea of the presidency was quite ripe by the time of the spring session of the Supreme Soviet and, as noted earlier, was on the agenda of the Third Congress of People's Deputies.

Opinions differed. Most members of the Supreme Soviet supported the idea of the presidency, but, in its most untenable form. To them, the presidency was a way to put things in order—the dream of "a strong arm" come true. That drew a powerful protest from democratic forces, in particular the Inter-Regional Group. I spoke against that approach to the Supreme Soviet. We did not need a Policeman of All Russia. We needed an arbitrator, a coordinator, and a head of executive power with personal responsibility for his decisions. In other words, we needed a personification of both power and responsibility, for so long as we were ruled by collegiate bodies no one was accountable.

In a law-governed society, generation of law should not be rested in an individual. Executive authority is a different matter.

The Inter-Regional Group met several days before the opening of the Third Congress and adopted the following resolution:

> Our position is the following. Although we consider, in principle, that the presidency is a progressive form of government compared with what we have now, the question of the President of the USSR and the procedure of his election should not be decided in haste, without the participation of the new Supreme Soviets of the Republics, without a developed multi-party system in the country, without a free press or without strengthening the present Supreme Soviet. The question should be coordinated with the constitutions of the republics and the new Union Treaty. If a decision on the presidency is adopted without observing these indispensable conditions, this will undoubtedly lead to greater tension between the Center and the republics, to the limiting of the independence of the local Soviets and self-government, and to the danger of the restoration of a dictatorial regime in the country . . .
>
> If Mikhail Gorbachev is elected President of the USSR, the interregional group of deputies will nominate Anatoly Sobchak for the post of Chairman of the USSR Supreme Soviet.

When the extraordinary Third Congress of People's Deputies was convened in March 1990, the presidency was the central item on the agenda. Debate centered on two main questions.

How should the president be elected? Everybody had agreed that presidential power was necessary. Paralysis of the executive government was all too obvious. The democratic forces insisted on countrywide elections.

Should the President remain General Secretary? Could the combination of the two offices benefit democratization?

My position had been somewhat different from that adopted by the democratic camp, from the first discussion within the Inter-Regional Group, in the Supreme Soviet and, later, in the Congress. Although I favored the presidency and stronger executive government, I felt it was inexpedient to institute the office of president at the Congress.

This position seemed half-hearted to many, and, in the final analysis, it suited neither the government nor the democrats. But I still think I was correct. At the Congress we should have invested Gorbachev with full presidential powers. But until the new constitution was adopted, he should have retained the post of Chairman of the USSR Supreme Soviet.

Why?

Presidential elections should, of course, be nationwide. Only then will the president enjoy the country's confidence. There was also an additional consideration which both political analysts and journalists failed to see, although I thought I had formulated it quite coherently both in the Supreme Soviet and in the Inter-Regional Group.

If we had elected a President then (either at the Congress or in a countrywide election, it made no difference), he would not have been interested in adopting a new constitution. We would have hastily created the office of president, our head of state would have received a quite civilized title, and yet the adoption of a new constitution would have been put off indefinitely.

However, if we had invested the chairman of the Supreme Soviet with the full range of presidential powers *temporarily* until the new constitution was adopted and countrywide presidential elections were held, Gorbachev—who was a shoo-in for the post—would have hastened the drafting and adoption of the constitution. And this meant that we would have had the chance to come to grips with the destructive processes in our country.

Alas, I was a voice in the wilderness. Gorbachev rejected my proposal, saying, "We don't need that." The proposal was neither discussed nor put to the vote. Anatoly Lukyanov's remarkable gift for selective deafness to calls for votes on some issues was again confirmed. Actually, I think Gorbachev understood better than anyone the sense of what I had said. But he preferred the easier and quicker way of getting presidential powers. It was understandable; the 29th Party Congress was approaching, its outcome unpredictable. The old party structures were breaking out of their stasis and gearing up for battle.

My misgivings came true. It was a long time before the Constitutional Commission met again. The parallel power structure remained, and created a vicious circle that put a stranglehold on Gorbachev. Gorbachev won tactically, but lost strategically. The result remained to be seen.

The Extraordinary Third Congress

The radical democrats were in full outcry. Support for the presidency came from such orthodox politicians as the first secretary of the Krasnodar party committee Ivan Polozkov, and Air Force Marshal Ivan Kozheduh, representing war veterans and Heroes of the Soviet Union.

An extract from Polozkov's statement is illustrative of the collective enthusiasm:

> We have all witnessed the creation of the law on cooperatives, and now we have learned from the mass media why People's Deputies Tikhonov and Sobchak pushed it through . . . Money, it turns out, is a fascinating thing, and greed has never been harmless. We do have a parliamentary and press cooperative lobby, no matter how hard people might try to deny it. That lobby now has a law that it likes and mass media, money and, consequently, real power. Anyone who stands in the way of this national and international mafia . . . experiences daily the weight of massive pressure, blackmail, and threats that extend even to physical coercion. (Ivan Polozkov later apologized for these words to Academician Tikhonov and me at the Deputies' Ethics Commission.)

Polozkov ends:

> . . . Dear Russian colleagues, doesn't it pain you today to see what liberties are now taken with Russia, that its long-suffering heroic people are being ridiculed? Their history is being distorted, the roots of their culture are being cut off, their values are being called into question. I appeal to you to vote for presidential power, and I believe that under such conditions there will be social justice and protection for nationalities, including the Russian people.

Marshal Kozhedub followed soon after Polozkov:

> It is with great pain and anxiety that we witness the growing attempts of extremist, anti-Soviet forces to . . . destroy the foundations of the Soviet system. It is time to go onto the offensive against the counter-revolutionary forces. Delay may mean death.

But majority support for *the presidency* did not mean that the majority was striving for *democracy*.

That was the most critical moment in the work of the crisis-filled Third Congress. It was the most perilous moment Gorbachev had faced in the five years of democratic change. The deputies resolved that before determining how the president should be elected, it was necessary to decide whether to allow the posts of president and general secretary to be combined.

The constitutional amendments introducing the presidency into the country's fundamental law had already been adopted. It would be to the distinct advantage of the right-wingers—Ligachev's crew—if the presidency were to be definitely split off from party work, making the president a mere figurehead. Real power would flow into the hands of the orthodox Marxists. In other words, the division of the presidency and party posts proposed by several left-wing deputies would strip Gorbachev of power and oust him from the Politburo, with disastrous implications for the future of the country and the entire process of democratization. It was a trap the radical democrats overlooked.

But the neo-Stalinists spotted it right away.

The mood was clearly against combining the posts. There was an electricity in the air that shouted, No! Gorbachev could see which way the vote was going to go.

The chairman cut short the discussion. The amendment was put to the vote: "The person elected to the post of President of the USSR shall not hold any other political or government post." One minute and 45 seconds later, the electronic tabulator showed 1,303 deputies *for*, 607 *against* the Resolution. It was short of the necessary plurality (1,497). But two hundred or so more *yeas*, and the *ad hoc* alliance of neo-Stalinists and radical democrats would have won.

And a Pyrrhic victory it would have been. The party Congresses that lay ahead may have succeeded in setting back the clock.

A Sobering Look Ahead

The right-wingers' hopes had been raised—just one more blow, one more assault, and what Boris Gidaspov failed to achieve with his November 1989 "meeting putsch" may have been accomplished. We saw the conservatives gathering their forces.

Gorbachev, who seldom made tactical errors, slipped when a well-known cosmonaut suggested a provision that the president of the

USSR not be permitted to hold another paid office. Gorbachev took off on the subject of his earnings:

"We have to sort things out here. For instance, I'm holding two posts now, I'm still receiving the salary of Politburo members, 1200 rubles. I've never drawn the salary designated for the chairman of the USSR Supreme Soviet, nor, of course, am I about to do so."

He wanted to make the point that he was not getting two salaries, but was "living on his wages and nothing else." But what he got for his trouble was noisy discontent. Gorbachev must have been embarrassed; he cut off a deputy reaching for the microphone and said, "Too many questions. We must move ahead."

On a great many of our minds was the question: who's in charge here? The party, or the government structures? Were we still ruled by a General Secretary paid at the Politburo who considered himself a Politburo employee? Was his position as chairman of the Supreme Soviet just a sideline—volunteer work?

Going over the Congress proceedings, I realized it must have been the shock from the close vote that so shook Gorbachev. What was on his mind? It was not hard to guess. Fewer than a third of the deputies voted for Gorbachev's line. Had he any hope of getting a majority on his side for president?

Did not the radical democrats see this? Ligachev and Co. certainly did.

The Congress was offended; the presidium was mocking them. There was an atmosphere of rather childish resentment, a sense of hurt pride.

This all could have been avoided had Gorbachev agreed to *temporary* investiture of presidential powers pending adoption of the constitution and a general election. But he wanted insurance, because his national popularity was waning, while Yeltsin's seemed to be increasing by the hour. (Vladislav Starkov, editor of *Argumenty i fakty* [Arguments and Facts], the country's most popular weekly, almost lot his job for publishing a popularity poll based on readers' letters.)

Many deputies began taking a tough attitude towards Gorbachev. The voters had not empowered us to elect a president. National debates and elections were needed.

A deputy from a small industrial center near Gorky cited data from a mini-referendum held on March 4. Out of 17,000 people polled in his constituency, 13,000 were in favor of district countrywide elections, and only 3,700 favored electing a President at the Congress. That was 75 percent in favor of nationwide elections.

"I think you would have gotten the same result in your constituency if you had conducted a similar poll," the deputy told the Congress.

It was impossible to argue.

The only thing to do was to pass over it in silence, ignore it.

A Crisis

I was busy with the drafting commission, casting my lawyer's eye over draft resolutions and doing some editing. We met in the backstage rooms where the presidium members relaxed during breaks.

Political gossip was rife. "Have you heard . . . ?" attracted enough information-swappers to fill the whole space.

Someone heard that Gorbachev said he would resign if not elected. Dead silence—then a furious discussion ensued. Who would replace him? A string of names was reeled off, starting with Nikolai Ryzhkov.

These were players in the political stock market. The shares of one politician go down, the shares of others rise. It was a hectic day for them.

I just watched. Nobody paid any attention to me. I got a birds-eye view of the whole political game. It was enough to send a chill down your spine.

A fellow liberal came up to me.

"Have you heard about the possible resignation? Do you know who they want as a replacement?"

"Yes, unfortunately."

"If we allow Gorbachev to lose at the Congress, we'll plunge the country into chaos!"

I agreed completely. It took at least two to three months to prepare a national presidential election. Electoral commissions had to be set up, polling stations prepared, paperwork, ballots readied . . . The country could be left without a head of state, while Gorbachev's unofficial power as leader would be gone as well.

Power would revert to the party. The death knell of democracy would be sounded.

Given the alignment of forces in the Central Committee, it would have been easy enough to oust the ex-leader from the Politburo as well. (Gorbachev never had majority backing in the Central Committee.)

Democrats had often called Gorbachev a hostage to the Central Committee, saying that as a deputy from the Communist Party he could be recalled by a plenary session of the Central Committee (and thus lose the post of chairman of the USSR Supreme Soviet). We were on the verge of doing the same thing ourselves, only in a different, "democratic" way.

We decided to skip lunch and talk to the deputies, especially those whose parliamentary and personal prestige might influence the Congress and salvage matters.

During the break, I managed to get assurances of support from some leaders of the Inter-Regional Group; I had to swallow some reproaches for my opposition to the group's decision to press for a nationwide presidential election. But I argued consistently that we should not wait for the adoption of the new constitution before investing Gorbachev with presidential powers. What would happen if a severe parliamentary crisis were precipitated? The Inter-Regional radicals would have managed to split the country into two antagonistic camps.

Democrats setting off a counterrevolution? Was it possible? Of course it was—if political amateurism, vestiges of demagogy, and an inability to calculate the simplest consequences of one's actions had not yet yielded to a sense of historical perspective and professionalism. To paint pictures, bake bread, teach, or heal, people need both natural ability and professional skill. In the initial stages of democracy, mere allegiance to the democratic camp was enough to earn someone a hero's laurels. But, there are horses for war and horses for parades. We, the first generation, are bound to look like self-taught amateurs to our children and grandchildren. It is nothing to brag about.

Back to March 14. I approached the distinguished elderly Academician Dmitri Likhachev and asked him to consider saying something after the break.

Voices

I managed to get the floor, and said:

> . . . The bottomline of what practically everyone has said is that today we are faced with a paralysis of government. We have adopted a de-

cision on changing Articles 6 and 7 of the USSR Constitution, which means dismantling that system of government, in essence a Party government, where the Party came to replace the state. Naturally, under these conditions there can be no instant change, no instant transition of the government from one state to another. All this will need time.

Now let us stop to think whether the theoretically correct and irreproachable provision of having a President elected by the country's entire population can be put into practice, given our present conditions. On the other hand, there is the undoubted paralysis of executive power, on the other, we have a situation where there is a state of emergency in a number of regions and where a number of state formations within the USSR have adopted unilateral decisions on secession from the Union. I remind you of the decisions taken by the Nakhichevan Autonomous Republic, the Lithuanian Republic, and the message of Estonia's Congress . . . Each nation within our Union has the right to secede and to make an independent decision on its statehood. But, I repeat, only within the framework of the law, only in a constitutional manner. As it is, today I do not see any other way of solving the problem other than the election of the first President of the Congress of People's Deputies of the USSR. I shall vote for such a solution and I appeal to all of you to do likewise.

My ally of earlier in the day, Nikolai Travkin, also ascended the rostrum:

I also have something to say on the motives for voting. First, the reasons dictated by common sense and then those prompted by some human considerations.

I do not understand the logic of the republics. When they raise the question of leaving the Soviet Union, they think it is enough to hold a session at home, adopt decisions, send in a piece of paper, and then make out they have seceded. I cannot believe this is serious. I believe that the mechanism of secession should be negotiations and the establishment of new economic and trade relations. Whom will the republic find it easier to talk to—the Supreme Soviet, this Congress, or President Gorbachev? . . .

Second, Ministerial banditry has gone quite far enough. All the sprouts of the market economy have been smothered. The process of strangling cooperatives, commercial banks, and joint ventures is coming to an end. The lease was crushed before it had time to get out of its cradle.

Ministers, members of the government, are making profit on the side by trading in tanks. We have already spoken about this. Deputies from the CPSU conclude foreign trade deals, and people's control bodies punish them for a multi-million loss in foreign currency by imposing fines which amount to triple their salaries. Will the Supreme Soviet be able to stop this economic depravity and banditry? No, it will not. It can only be stopped by a man invested with personal responsibility, someone who has this responsibility breathing down his neck. This is the second reason why the President should be elected here, at the Congress, but only for a term of three years.

Third. It would be very nice to elect a President in a nationwide election, nice and democratic, and I am all for it. One need not forego one's principles and one can insist on it. But it seems to me the situation in the country is such that a much smaller number of people will be taking part in the election—the survivors. We are on the brink of a civil war. Look how many trouble zones we have. Can we wait? I don't think we can.

These are the three reasons that compel me to appeal to my democratic brethren to vote today. But there is also another reason, a purely human one. I put myself in Gorbachev's place, in his place as merely a human being. The situation is like this: I am considered a scoundrel because I am striving for power, but I am a human being and I have my self-respect. The moment will come when I will say: I've had enough. You don't trust me? Then sort it all out yourselves. Frankly, such a thought unnerves me. During lunch Sobchak and myself both became unnerved by the very idea, knowing only too well that since we are dealing with human beings, we may find ourselves dealing with one of the people who made a long speech here yesterday, a Party leader . . .

I appeal to you once again, let us forego our "principles," otherwise in what way shall we differ from those we criticize? (Noise in the hall.)

He was followed by Moscow deputy Ilya Zaslavsky:

My voters have also instructed me to vote for a nationwide election. I appeal to you to vote in accordance with the constitution, as befits deputies. Let each of us vote the way his conscience tells him.

Sergei Zalygin, editor of the magazine *Novy Mir*, followed:

I cannot imagine what the purpose behind our extraordinary Congress is if the question of electing the President of the USSR is not solved the way, for instance, deputies Sobchak and Travkin suggest. History will not forgive us if we fail to take advantage of this last chance. (Applause.)

Nikolai Panov, aircraft commander:

Comrades, we are not only deputies, we must also be politicians, and this means we must foresee the future and be accountable for the consequences of the decisions we are going to adopt at this Congress . . .

This preamble was perfectly correct. However, in real life the desire and the ability to be a politician are two things that not always coincide. Deputy Panov had just one argument, and he failed to hear anything else:

In our society, in the society where one lighted match can blow the whole of our system to smithereens, where the nationalities question has come to a head, we can lose simply by failing to give all Soviet people the right to take part in elections directly.

I was reluctant to offend a fellow democrat, but that was typical parliamentary defeatism.

Next to speak was Alexander Yakovlev, a member of the Politburo, and Gorbachev's closest and most consistent supporter. We shall be forever indebted to him for his analytic ability and civic courage.

Let us not ignore the past we tend to forget so quickly. We must also take into account the fact that a nationwide vote will be much more democratic under a multi-party system. In the meantime, I am deeply convinced that the logic of perestroika is speeding ahead and pushing us on. In effect, the struggle between those forces which firmly adhere to the policies of perestroika and those forces set against it is now in a decisive phase. Things are far from over . . . Don't let us play hide-and-seek. The matter in hand today is the election of a specific leader, Mikhail Gorbachev, to the post of the country's President. It seems that almost everybody agreed with that. So according to what scale of justice and morality do we try on this extremely heavy "crown of Monomach," so to speak, only to shove it into a dusty storeroom afterwards? One cannot die twice or be born twice. We should give this some thought. But if someone is busy looking for a new leader, here too, dear comrades, we should think seriously both about the motives and consequences of such a step. There is no going back for us, and even if there were, it would be disastrous. The introduction of the presidency is a transition of fundamental importance from collective vagueness to personal responsibility. For each of us it is an historical opportunity to show some personal responsibility and personal wisdom. (*Applause*)

I was sure that Gorbachev would not deny Dimitri Likhachev the right to address the Congress, since Likhachev seldom asked for the floor. But I was not at all sure that an eighty-year-old man would be willing to plunge headlong into parliamentary battle. All the more so, since he wasn't apt to make any friends by speaking out. (Indeed, to this day, some radical democrats hold Likhachev's words at the Congress against him.) But I heard with delight: "The floor is given to Deputy Likhachev, Dmitri Sergeyevich."

The old-fashioned Russian courtesy of addressing or introducing someone by first name and patronymic was unusual at our congresses. Gorbachev preferred party-style informality, which had been known to ruffle some deputies' feathers. But Likhachev was a special case, not just because he was a grey-haired academician, but because of his great personal and civic prestige. Gorbachev called Sakharov "Andrei Dmitrievich," and at the September 1990 session of the Supreme Soviet he referred to "that great man, Alexander Isayevich Solzhenitsyn." (Although he criticized sharply Solzhenitsyn's book on the future of Russia.)

LIKHACHEV'S WORDS

Dear comrades, I am not a lawyer, but it seems to me that I am the oldest deputy in this hall. I have a perfect memory of the February revolution, so I know what popular emotions mean, and I must tell you that at present our country is in the grip of emotions. In these conditions direct presidential elections will actually lead to a civil war. Believe me and trust my experience. That is why I am against a direct election. The election should be made here and now. It must not be postponed. This is the first thing.

Second. The question arises regarding the alleged need to divide Party and government power. If we divide it, we shall deny Party power to the President, thus creating opposition to the government and also leading the country into civil war. This is intolerable. We all want strong power now, and that is why we should not divide power. (*Applause.*)

It was a superb example of parliamentary address—not a superfluous word. It was as exact as a mathematical proof (although Dmitri Likhachev was a scholar of the humanities, not a mathematician), and emotionally telling as well. It was Dimitri Likhachev who captured the swing vote that day, and to whom, in my view, Gorbachev owed his presidency. (A little more than half the deputies went on to cast their votes for Gorbachev in the secret ballot.)

About fifty percent of the deputies voted to adopt the third and fourth sections. The apparat's opposition to Gorbachev apparently comprised something approaching 20-25 percent of the deputies. These were the people who flattered the leader to his face while secretly anticipating the return of the good old days. Their actions were well-coordinated. Their bureaucratic experience enabled them to maintain "Party discipline." By this, I mean not adherence to the official party line, but a "shadow discipline" by which they sought to preserve their power and promote their own "class" interests.

The more moderate group of democrats included many people who had public reputations before the First Congress of People's Deputies as scientists, writers, journalists, etc.; that is, with some political sophistication. Political professionalism and the ability to calculate the long-term consequences of decisions generally go hand in hand. Professionals tend to be more pragmatic and flexible. Opposition on principle easily becomes fruitless sophomoric rebellion, and, thus in the long run, results in the loss of the strategic objective.

Of course, a great deal depended on temperament, stature, and personal and social circumstances of individual deputies. For instance, those who came to the democratic camp from within the system and those who failed to make the grade professionally in their former pursuits were inclined to take the toughest line. Still, it's risky to generalize.

Overall, it was safe to say that democrats were far more open and sensitive than the apparat activists. The democrats might have given the president a lot of trouble, but they were far less dangerous than treacherous apparatchiks who were ever ready to betray, abandon, or replace any leader who no longer suited them.

The Turning Point

Dmitri Likhachev's statement was a turning point. The mood in the hall changed; the Congress had been convinced; the specter of civil war no longer haunted the assembly. Things had been called by their real names. The ghost had vanished as quickly as it appeared.

Journalists have noted that Gorbachev's victories have all had similar scenarios. Each time, he picked himself up after a real stumble. His adversaries were sure they had done the trick, making Gorbachev political dead meat. But it was at that very juncture that he inevitably made his decisive and incredibly powerful thrust.

It is hard to say how much of this was tactical and how much was dictated by the internal logic of battle. Western political analysts used to call Brezhnev's "hypochondria" tactical maneuvering, but the ailments were very real. People, especially our country's, are accustomed to view their rulers as playing cunning games, exercising inhuman logic and behavior, and whims. It is a hangover from the superstitious awe that once surrounded the tsar. Seven decades of Soviet power have only strengthened these mythological structures in the people's consciousness.

Meanwhile, a leader is a human being, with all his weaknesses and passions. Gorbachev understood better than anyone the seriousness of the situation at the Congress on March 13 and 14, 1990. I know for a fact that he was forced to seek medical attention. This was not advertised because at such moments the man at the top is not supposed to show any sign of physical weakness. As things were, Gorbachev could not even turn to the Kremlin doctors (evidently, he realized he would be taken to the hospital). Instead, he asked one of the deputies for aid.

However, he did not permit himself either requests for help or any negotiations with the leaders of deputies' groups. This is conduct deserving respect. The candidate for the presidency himself knew that those people supported him not because he was a candle in the dark, nor out of respect for his numerous merits, and not even because, as Gorbachev himself once said, one should not change horses in midstream. I emphasize again that most of the democratic deputies supported not so much Gorbachev the man, as the ideas inseparably linked with his name.

I hope Gorbachev realized this. But he must also realize that it was, as Andrei Sakharov once put it, "conditional support," and that the condition was the course of perestroika and the entire effort to dismantle communist totalitarianism.

After the vote for President, many deputies chided me for getting involved in a parliamentary squabble at the Congress, for taking on the prime minister over the ANT mess, and for clashing with Ivan Polozkov, the rising star of orthodox communism. Some of the deputies decided that Sobchak was busy making his own career in the Supreme Soviet and was aspiring to the post of chairman of the Supreme Soviet.

As a matter of fact, what I heard in the corridors of the Palace of Congresses was: "Look what you have done? We wanted to vote for you!"

On the eve of the Third Congress, the Inter-Regional Group had decided to vote against introducing the presidency. If it were instituted, the group decided (after rather heated discussion) to unanimously recommend deputy Sobchak for the country's second most important government post. I retorted that if we wanted to kill off democracy in our land, we could do no better than to propose Yeltsin, Afanasyev, or Sobchak: the apparat could still endure Gorbachev, but if any of us were elected, it would trigger a coup d'état, if not a full-scale military putsch.

Everyone agreed. As things stood, it would have been strange if the Inter-Regional Group, opposed to the presidency in principle, had nominated its own man for the job.

So, by the will of fate, and not by my own volition, I became Anatoly Lukyanov's rival and a claimant to the country's number two government office. I found myself in a very delicate situation among my fellow democrats. I realized that I stood a real chance of being elected chairman—all I had to do was to keep my mouth shut.

I told Gavril Popov that I was going to speak out.

My sharp-witted colleague suggested a brilliant bit of verbal tactics; I thanked him, and said goodbye to temptation. There would be no seat for me among the leaders of the Supreme Soviet. I could not forego my own freedom as a deputy.

Neither in Moscow nor in Leningrad had the intelligentsia ever been all that delighted about Boris Yeltsin. But it seemed that Yeltsin, having surrounded himself with a clever team, was proving capable of learning from mistakes, both his own and Gorbachev's. The chairmen of a number of republic soviets* hastened to acquire the status of president in summer 1990, but Yeltsin bided his time. This only increased the voters' confidence in him.

The country's political atmosphere was shifting rapidly. An editor was no longer threatened with expulsion from the party and

* Governors of states would be the closest U.S. analogy—*ed.*

the loss of his job for publishing a public opinion poll. A multi-party system was permitted. Censorship had been abolished. But society was now embroiled in even more serious and dangerous problems.

If it were only a simple fall in the popularity of one political leader, and growing popular affection for the other! Alas, 1990 saw interethnic tragedy in the Caucasus, war between Armenia and Azerbaijan, bloodshed in Moldavia, and skirmishes between the Union and Russian Federation parliaments. The atmosphere of confrontation between Yeltsin and Gorbachev was unsettling. The final blow came when the "500 days" economic program was adopted by Russia but torpedoed by the central government.

Much of this came about as a direct or indirect result of electing a president at the Third Congress of People's Deputies. Politicians' mistakes mean tears and bloodshed for their fellow citizens. On November 7, 1990, a man carrying a sawed-off shotgun attempted to assassinate Gorbachev in Red Square. *Moscow News* carried a photograph taken during the November 7, 1989 civic parade in a town in Leningrad's administrative region, in which the attempted assassin could be seen standing under a handmade poster declaring: "For direct, contested nationwide elections of the head of state!" Twelve months later, this self-described "democrat" would pull out a double-barreled shotgun squarely in front of the Mausoleum viewing stand.

About a decade ago, just after my marriage, I became involved in gathering material on the interrogation of the Decembrists and their trial. My wife, Lyudmila, was writing her thesis on these early revolutionaries, and thanks to her, I began to take a keen interest in that period of Russian history. I wanted to take a closer look at an early example of Russia's judicial laxity from a lawyer's point of view. I wanted to show that there was method to arbitrary rule and a certain logic behind the contradictory sentences handed down by the government on the entire generation of the first democrats in our country. I never got around to writing a book on it, but I still have several frayed folders with notes on the subject, and I hope to return to it some day. Perhaps I will manage to show how dangerous totalitarianism was to the rulers of Russia, and how they themselves were sawing away at the then-flourishing tree of Russian statehood.

I think that the lawyer Gorbachev is just as well versed in Russian history as the lawyer Sobchak, and I don't have to remind the President of the USSR that even the best political decision is correct only when it is made at the right moment. Delayed, it may boomerang instead . . .

In early autumn 1990, talking with Moscow's mayor, Gavril Popov, I happened to remark on the upcoming November 7 holiday (perhaps "holiday" was a misnomer, since the anniversary of the Bolshevik Revolution was no longer treated as a festive occasion by many of my fellow countrymen). It was clear that November 7, 1990, was going to be a difficult day. Opposition groups in the Baltic republics, Georgia, and Russia's largest cities were certain to make a show of force. What if it were to become a repetition of November 7, 1917?

Popov promptly suggested a joint press conference at which the mayors of the two largest Russian cities would call upon local councils and citizens to refrain from demonstrations or rallies. We hoped this would apply as well to the president, for at the time even a traditional military parade might have triggered a bloodbath.

We asked, "What should we have instead of the military review and civil parade?"

Popov evidently had prepared a reply in advance.

"Let's propose holding a day of preparation for winter. You know what our country's like after the first frosts set in."

We held a press conference and read out our joint statement. We also sent a memo to the president—he would read it in the press, of course, but we wanted to do things strictly by the book.

The answer was not long in coming. A few days later, I opened a newspaper and read a presidential decree announcing that a military review would take place.

This came during troubled days when there were alarming rumors of an impending military coup. In the country's parliament, democratic deputies spoke up about paratroop units moving into an area close to Moscow. The generals dismissed this as the need to prepare for the parade and help farmers with the harvest. Few believed that paratroopers in full combat gear and bulletproof jackets had been brought in to dig potatoes, and the president himself came to the rescue of the army's honor.

The chairman of the Leningrad city council—the mayor—has a direct telephone link with the President of the USSR. There was

nothing left but for me to get on the hotline. The President's secretary put me through immediately. I repeated the arguments Popov
and I had advanced and asked Gorbachev to reconsider.

Gorbachev rejected my arguments out of hand. November 7 was
an official holiday, there was constitutional provision for it, the people
expected a parade. He had on his desk thousands of messages from
citizens urging him not to yield to Popov's and Sobchak's statement.
"I consider your joint statement politically mistaken and advise you
not to make such statements in the future," he ended.

I countered that I could not guarantee public security during the
military review and the civil parade in Leningrad. There was also a
problem regarding the use of troops to maintain order during the
review. After Tbilisi, the minister of defense had issued an order
forbidding the use of troops for such purposes.

Gorbachev replied that he would talk it over with Marshal
Yazov, and that a number of troops would be detailed to see that the
review proceeded according to schedule. The units would be with-
drawn immediately after the review and take no part in keeping order
during the civil parades.

Well, that was something, at least. One did not have to be a
genius to guess that the radical left and extremist groups would try to
interfere with the review.

That was exactly what happened. In Leningrad, the command-
ing general of the military district ordered the armored units to spend
the preceding night in Palace Square; otherwise, they would not have
been able to get in: people were planning to lie down under the
wheels of armored personnel carriers.

The Leningrad review took place. The militia cordon barred the
pickets from the square. There was an unpleasant incident when a
group of teenagers, along with two or three deputies of the Leningrad
city council, broke through to Alexander Garden from Senate Square.
The militia tore down their placards and pushed them out by force.
Of course, when the military review was over, these people returned
to the square. Gidaspov was now holding a communist rally attended
by a conspicuously small audience. His official declaration that "the
holiday could not be abolished" failed to spark much enthusiasm. A
rota of professional speakers urged the audience not to forego their
principles and to "stand firm." Meanwhile, a scuffle broke out below
the podium, and the Russian tricolor and the Red flag clashed—
literally.

As it turned out, there were no casualties. But when an alternative rally was held by the social democratic parties and organizations in the same square a few hours later, those watching TV saw, perhaps for the first time, the burning of the state flag.

Newspapermen called the day "a festival of confrontation." Did the burning of the hammer and sickle in Leningrad's Palace Square and the attempt to assassinate Gorbachev add to the president's prestige? In the capital of Georgia, the military review had to be moved to a drill ground (hardly a holiday event!). The same had to be done in the Baltic republics.

In Leningrad, the decision was made to give a public demonstration of how naval ships weigh anchor and leave the Neva river. "Glasnost," military-style, turned to humiliation when the very first ship (which with poetic justice bore the name *Smolny*, Lenin's headquarters of the proletarian revolution), turning about, hit the pier of a bridge named after Lieutenant Schmidt, the hero of the 1905 Revolution.

The word went around the city afterward that it was no coincidence that a brass band on the Neva embankment had been playing a song about a cruiser sunk in the Russo-Japanese war, a line of which goes: "The last parade is beginning . . ."

If we are to become a law-governed society, the 1990 review should indeed be *the last parade*. The symbol of national might is not missiles or goosesteps shaking the ancient flagstones of the squares. To me, a civilian, bringing armored units into our own cities under cover of night and under the guard of special forces fails to add either honor or glory to an army for which I feel sincere respect.

Meetings with President Gorbachev are as a rule brief, businesslike, and devoted to specific issues. Of late, we have concentrated on Leningrad's problems (alas, our system is such that many things still have to be done through the chief executive).

Gorbachev is a man who knows how to listen. He pays attention and his mien encourages you to state your case in detail.

I don't know about others, but I have always tried to do so concisely and with precision. The president never seemed to rush me. His remarks draw you into conversation, you begin to forget about time and his heavy schedule and, having fallen under his hypnotic charm, you start talking about things you did not intend to bring up.

And at the same time you never know what this man, who is listening to you so attentively, is thinking about.

Gorbachev remains a mystery to me.

He may agree with your arguments and you leave confident you have convinced him. But it would be unwise to jump to conclusions. The decision he makes may be based not on your arguments, but on others quite unknown to you. Thus, there is always an element of unpredictability.

He never bares himself to the person he is talking to, and there has never been an occasion when anyone of my fellow deputies to the Supreme Soviet could say: I know what Gorbachev is really like. This also applies to Gorbachev's statements in the Supreme Soviet in which emotion has obviously overridden calculation.

Twice, I have experienced a splash of Gorbachev's emotions. If one recalls that in both cases, the issue involved the authority of the head of state, one might conclude that power is Gorbachev's most vexing problem. Paradoxical as it may seem, this is not proof of a "lust for power" in political terms, for, in a state not governed by law, pure power does determine the destiny of the head of state and, as often as not, the whole country. So if you think that you have solved the Gorbachev enigma, think again.

During the decades of his ascent in the communist hierarchy Gorbachev learned the apparat's structure. This immense impersonal construct still awaits its Dante. Gorbachev could tell us much we do not know about how a man feels, doomed to daily renunciation of his own will in favor of that of his superiors, compelled to daily self-abasement for the sake of his career.

Significantly, in his youth, Gorbachev used to walk more than seven kilometers to attend the rehearsals of an amateur drama troupe. I think that theatrical experience stood him in good stead both as a bureaucrat and as a person.

Gorbachev started his fight against the system, putting forward the idea of a law-governed state at the very beginning of perestroika. He attacked the very heart of the system after he had been elevated to the top of the party hierarchy. The idea of perestroika followed logically from the notion of a law-governed state, combined with Gorbachev's declared priority of human over class values, as did the ideas of glasnost and pluralism. He added to them a multi-party political system, parliamentarianism, a varied economy, with private property the basis of individual freedom and social security for citizens.

Mikhail Gorbachev taking the oath as President of the USSR in March 1990

Sobchak visiting the Chicago Board of Trade during a trip to the United States

Sobchak with Yeltsin on a visit to the Greek parliament

On one of many flights from Leningrad to Moscow

Telman Gdlyan *(Right)*, co-head with Nikolai Ivanov of the investigative team examining corruption in Uzbekistan. Gdlyan, along with his colleague, was charged by Procurator General Sukharev with alleged illegal practices. He became a People's Deputy of Armenia in part to retain parliamentary immunity from right-wing accusers.

Nikolai Ivanov, co-head of the deposed Uzbekistan investigative team, is also now a People's Deputy of Armenia and has continued to attack the Soviet judicial system as a bastion of apparat privilege and fraud.

Sobchak in the discussion of the law on property during the second session of the Supreme Soviet of the USSR

Just weeks before Boris Gidaspov's "meeting putsch" in November 1989, the Russian Communist Party rallied in Leningrad, uniting the old-line communists with younger right-wing nationalists and fascists.

(*Left*) Boris Gidaspov, the Leningrad city and regional party chief, defender of the apparat, and frequent opponent of Mayor Sobchak. Since the August 1991 coup and dissolution of the party organization, he is apparently unemployed. (*Right*) Nikolai Ryzhkov. The beleaguered prime minister suffered a heart attack in December 1990, following which Gorbachev named future coup leader Gennady Yennayev vice president. In March 1991, Ryzhkov ran unsuccessfully against Boris Yeltsin for the presidency of the Russian Federation.

(*Left*) Yegor Ligachev. A longtime party ideologue, he announced his retirement in July 1990 during the 28th Party Congress, to work on his memoirs. (*Right*) Ivan Polozkhov. A hardline head of Russia's Communist party and Yegor Ligachev's heir as number one conservative ideologue, he is now, presumably, unemployed.

Naval review in Leningrad in 1990

Commencement day, 1990, at the Leningrad Soviet military academy

Sobchak and Yeltsin with the patriarch of Moscow and all Russia, Alexi II, before the first services in the newly reopened St. Isaac's Cathedral

The museum becomes a cathedral, June 17, 1990

Sobchak addressing Yegor Ligachev at the 28th Party Congress

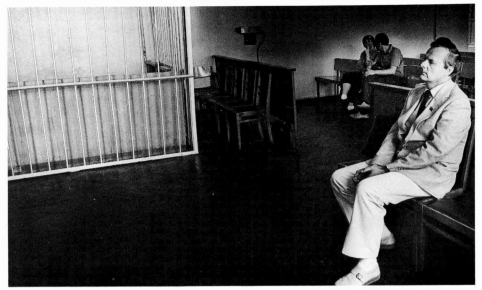

Sobchak waiting for no-show defendant Admiral Yegor Tomko, against whom Sobchak pressed a successful slander suit for Tomko's February 1990 newspaper accusations that he had "bought the vote" in Leningrad

On November 7, 1990, the Leningrad Popular Front demonstrated during the anniversary of the Bolshevik Revolution against right-wing forces. The "Democratic Russia" banner can be seen in the foreground.

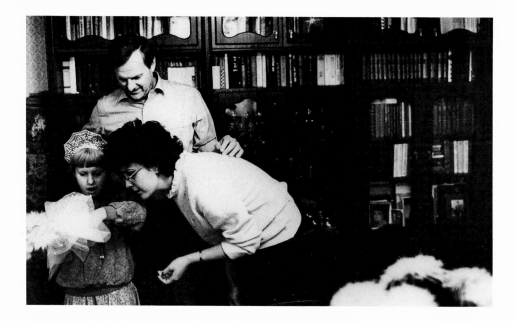

At home with the family

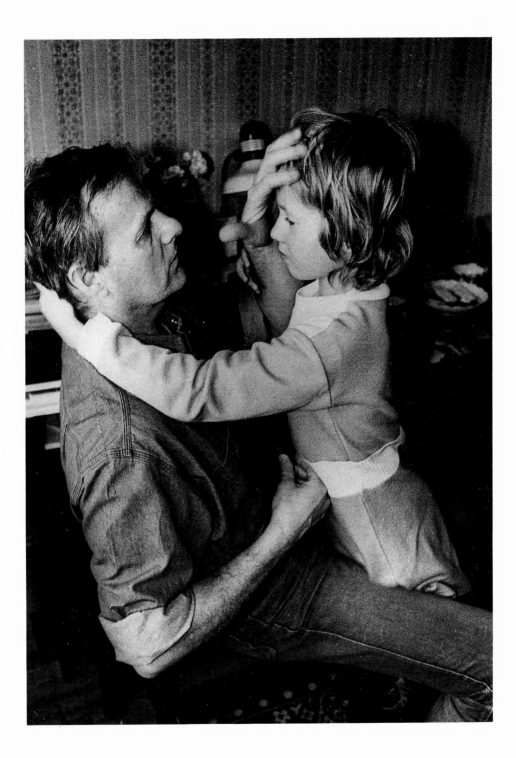

A brutal scene from Vilnius, as tanks crush civilians during the "bloody Sunday" massacre of January 1990

Citizens of Vilnius on their way to confront the Soviet military

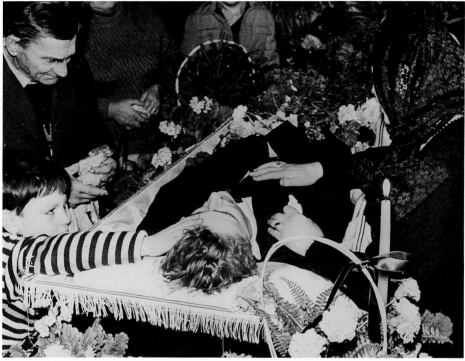

Mourners for the civilian dead in the aftermath of "bloody Sunday"

Sobchak responds to reporters' questions about the massacre in Vilnius (see Epilogue).

Revolution Square, St. Petersburg

Does this make Gorbachev the "traitor General Secretary" portrayed by the right wing? I believe one has to be either a zealot or a madman to retain faith in ideals for which mankind has paid such a terrible price. All over the world, communism has proved an inhuman regime. Communist labor has proved unproductive. Could it be that Gorbachev is a democrat who decided way back in his teens to fight against the utopia, a kind of "undercover agent" in the party camp? Part of our liberal intelligentsia initially thought so, but I'm dubious.

Another version held by many radical democrats has Gorbachev an ambitious dictator who is trying to replace one totalitarian system with another. A dictator, however, would not have started far-reaching changes, or tried to wake society from its communist lethargy. Dictators do not begin their ascent to power with democratic reforms that will place legal restraints on their omnipotence.

The way I see it, Gorbachev is a statesman, first and foremost. To him, both politics and ideology are simply means. And so is power itself.

Statesmen of his caliber always stand alone. They appear when there is social demand for a strong reformer, and, as a rule, they proceed from a deeprooted need for radical change and not from their commitment to some political ideology. Mikhail Gorbachev may have a personal soft spot for the communist worldview and for the historical figure of Lenin. But Gorbachev's personal ideological predilections are entirely his own business. They are far from determining his actions as a statesman. The left and the right are wasting their time trying to measure him by their own yardsticks. He is neither of the right nor of the left, neither a democrat nor a despot. He is Gorbachev.

In my childhood years we used to play a game called "King of the Castle." The boy who managed to stay on top of a snow hill became king. But no one stays on top for long in this game—you have to look sharp, for the slightest slip, and you are pushed off and roll down, covered in snow from head to foot. (The strongest and cleverest boys, realizing that their time is up, pick up a sled or a sheet of cardboard and slide down the hill of their own accord.)

Objectively, Gorbachev's role in history should not end before his reforms are done. Yet, if the necessary purely human, personal endurance falters, or if a series of errors in decisionmaking and political miscalculations result in the leader's stepping down, another leader will have to carry out the same reforms.

The paradox is that Gorbachev can neither hold together nor dissolve the Soviet empire. Years will have to pass before the republics establish free economic relations among themselves, before yesterday's inmates of the All-Union political and economic socialist camp learn the skills of free partnership. Yet it is these very *years* that we just do not have. A great deal hangs on a single individual's ability to pass the test of civic fortitude.

To me, the greatest mystery is how Gorbachev managed to retain his individuality, the ability to shape his own opinion and set it against the opinion of others. Evidently, it was to preserve his own self that he developed his almost impenetrable mask. He learned to conceal his disdain for those whom he must have despised, to speak with them in their own language.

And if this is so, is it easy, while communicating with him, to convince him by means of logic, especially if your argument takes place on your own intellectual territory, and not his?

Before our Tbilisi commission delivered its report to parliament, I had a face-to-face talk with Gorbachev. I told him that the military was demanding a supplementary report. To give the floor to the military prosecutor after the conclusions of the parliamentary commission would have cast contempt on Congress and doubt on the conclusions of the parliamentarians. Furthermore, if we had wanted to go that route, why shouldn't we have listened to someone from the leadership of the Republic of Georgia as well as the leadership of various unofficial Georgian political movements? After all, if we wanted to hold a discussion after the conclusions of the commission, if we wanted to get down to the truth right there, during a parliamentary hearing, we should have just done it.

Gorbachev seemed to agree. But . . . The military prosecutor got to make his supplementary report, and what I had predicted did occur: the Georgian delegation walked out in protest. Gorbachev had to spend the break between sessions persuading them to return. And Gorbachev himself, speaking to the Georgians, expressed his indignation over the prosecutor's arrogance and the lack of evidence in his report.

Gorbachev likes to say that he listens to everybody, but makes his decision independently. But there's another side to this laudable quality. For instance, Gorbachev chose the members of his Presidential Council in such a way that a few months later he himself realized that this body was unworkable, and was compelled to propose its dissolution in November 1990. It turned out that the obedience of the Presidential Council which, like Noah's Ark, had "two of each kind of all living creatures," was not the strength but the weakness of the President himself.

Such episodes demonstrated a desire on Gorbachev's part to preserve the balance of forces at all costs. This is a blessing in a stable and prosperous society. Every major politician must take the alignment of forces into account. But bureaucratic decisions and reshuffling of political cards are of no use at turning points in history, crises, times of trouble. A politician who forgets his strategic aim or is incapable of making a choice and directing society's "ark" to its proclaimed destination, is doomed.

In mid-November 1990, the members of the USSR Supreme Soviet for the first time staged what journalists called "a Kremlin revolt": both the left and the right refused to follow the agenda and demanded that Gorbachev report on the situation in the country.

For 24 hours, Gorbachev did not receive anyone as he prepared a report which the deputies found weak and disappointing. For the first time both the radical democrats and neo-Stalinists laughed at the leader in parliament. One of the deputies, Colonel Alksnis, even said threateningly that the President had "lost the army."

When my turn came to speak, I tried not to mince any words. The situation in the country was extraordinary and required extraordinary measures. There were only two ways out of the political crisis. The first was direct presidential rule with reliance on the army and punitive bodies. This way held no prospect for society. The second was to promote democratic changes coupled with strict measures to maintain law and order.

At that point, some of the deputies were already laughing at me, and I could not help but make the following observation: here is an example that shows how legal standards are poorly understood in our country, even in parliament. We still understand "order" the Stalinist way, and not the way it should be understood in democratic society—as observance of laws and strong executive power.

I said that if Gorbachev called for an offensive against those functionaries who were sabotaging perestroika and government decisions and against the type of extremists who burned our state flag at the November 7 parade, then we were with Gorbachev. But such an offensive was impossible without emergency measures to supply the country with food, without the government stopping the printing of

useless paper money, without handing over land to farmers and all
those wishing to take it, without privatization.

The wait-and-see attitude to which the President increasingly
seemed a hostage was dangerous. The alignments of political forces at
the top and bottom of society are never identical. In chess there is
such a thing as "losing the exchange."

In the summer of 1989, I had the "honor" of reading a joke about
myself in one of the Moscow weeklies:

> The Supreme Soviet is debating the question of private property. Gor-
> bachev, tired of the disputes, asks the deputies to take their seats
> according to their convictions. Those for socialism and against private
> property should sit on the left, those for private property and
> capitalism—on the right.
>
> Deputy Sobchak is the only one to rush about in the middle, not
> knowing which way to turn.
>
> "Well, Comrade Sobchak, why can't you make up your mind?"
>
> "You see, Mikhail Sergeyevich, I'm for socialism, but for living
> under it just as I would under capitalism."
>
> "In that case you should come here, to the presidium," said Gor-
> bachev.

Well, you cannot argue with a joke, unfair or not.

One day, a news photographer from one of the most conservative Soviet papers presented me with a picture taken at the 28th Party
Congress, saying: "You shouldn't think all of us are like our newspaper." The picture, which had been snapped with split-second timing,
showed Gorbachev and myself standing under a red banner, the
General Secretary holding me by the hand in a friendly and confi-
dential manner. The photo emanated patriarchal sentimentality, just
like the canvases of socialist realism in the 30s—that is, if one were
quite oblivious to the fact that a moment earlier Gorbachev had
learned that I had quit the party.

The aim of the reforms started by Mikhail Gorbachev is to build
a society as advanced as those of present-day Europe, in which the
attitude to capitalism or socialism would be the private business of a
free and well-fed people. If it turns out that for some reason Gorbachev cannot translate this idea into reality, we should nevertheless
carry on the effort of building a law-governed state and a free democratic society.

We internalized the dictatorship of the proletariat long ago.

Those who could not swallow it were destroyed with ruthless efficiency. Gorbachev started with the idea of building a law-governed state, and this single fact prompts faith that the process of renewing our life is irreversible. And, though he is far from being beyond criticism, the beginning of that process will always be associated with the name of Mikhail Gorbachev.

10

The End of Communism and the Birth of a New Russia

Nearly a hundred and fifty years ago, far off in Siberian exile, the Decembrist Mikhail Fonvizin wrote a prophetic article, "On Communism and Socialism." In it he said, "Attempts to realize such dreams threaten society with destruction, its reversion to savagery, and eventually a one-man dictatorship, as a consequence of anarchy."

This analysis of a future no one seriously expected was made by a revolutionary of noble origin some seventy years before the "Great October Revolution." "The weird fact, though perhaps unnoticed by many, is that Russia, an autocracy with a great deal of slavery, nonetheless contains the main element of socialistic and communistic theories," Fonvizin wrote. He added, "As the saying goes, 'extremes meet.'"

Such was the prophecy, now proved correct, by one of those whom Lenin considered extremely distant from the people. As the most right-wing newspapers are changing from red to brown, as the new national-socialists, monarchists, and fanatics act in unison, as a communist editor prints a eulogy to Ivan Polozkov side-by-side with the fabrication known as *The Protocols of the Elders of Zion* (calling it an authentic document), it becomes clear that from the ashes of communist ideology, already quite unpopular in Russia, the forces of evil do not just disappear.

Extremes meet. The anti-Semitic "patriots" and national-socialists, acting legally under the cover of Pamyat and other political groups which as yet have little power, are trying to form a bloc with the retreating communist structures, especially the official Russian Communist Party headed by Ivan Polozkov and the "ultra-loyalists" represented by the organizers of the RCP's Leningrad "founding congress" and groups like Nina Andreyeva's *Unity*.

The great Russian philosopher, Nikolai Berdyaev, viewed both Marx's collectivism and Nietzsche's extreme individualism as stemming from the crisis of humanism which had made *man* the leading force of history:

> Humanism is being directed against man and God. If there is nothing above man, if there is nothing higher than man, if man knows no other principles than those confined to the human circle, he ceases to know himself. What follows from the negation of divinity is that man fatally becomes subordinate to low, sub-human, not super-human, elements. This is the inevitable result of the entire path of Godless humanism in recent history . . . I am referring to Friedrich Nietzsche and Karl Marx. These two men, who never ever meet at any point, destroy humanism equally and pave the way for a transition to anti-humanism.

In the twentieth century, the "superman" idea gave the world fascism. Marxist collectivism produced the Bolshevik dream of global revolution and totalitarian regimes worldwide. When fascism and the fascist states collapsed in 1945, communist ideology seemed to set off on the victorious march across the globe that had not come to pass after World War I.

What has saved the world is not the atomic bomb or the Cold War, but human freedom and legal safeguards, both of which Lenin treated with distaste. They have enabled post-industrial society to defeat communist doctrine not by military action or the threat of the apocalypse, but by its social achievements.

In his book *Philosophy of Inequality*, Nikolai Berdyaev predicted:

> It would be impossible even to publish books, periodicals and news-papers freely, because all printing would be in the hands of a central collective, serving its interests and goals. . . The only thing to survive would be freedom of the unrealized spirit, and human spirit would become disembodied.

And this did come to pass. The nomenklatura was the "central collective," and the disembodiment of the spirit was the price of its omnipotence.

The decades of communist totalitarianism have left all too visible a trace in the souls of my fellow countrymen. The intelligentsia must do everything in its power to prevent another tide of totalitarianism—this time, overtly fascist—from engulfing the country. Otherwise, the world will stand little chance of survival.

I don't consider myself an anti-communist, for it is absurd to fight a ghost of the past. I do, however, count myself an anti-fascist.

The issue of private property lies at the heart of communist doctrine. Democrats and orthodox communists have crossed swords over this issue at every Congress of People's Deputies and Supreme Soviet session.

Since October 1917, we have been told repeatedly that private property is tantamount to exploitation. The rhetoric has never varied. Now, for the first time in more than seventy years, proponents of private property have been able to argue with communists face to face. They say that private property has proved efficient, that respect for the human being begins with recognition of his rights of ownership; and that in this country, a family can work hard all life long and still face an impoverished old age. Even the apartment in which they have lived for, let's say, fifty years, belongs to the state. They are not permitted to buy it. Our citizens are allowed to possess little more than a Roman slave—and far less than a Russian serf.

Years ago, Marxists believed that by abolishing private property the human race would rid itself of exploitation and live an ideal life in fraternity and equality. Alas, our society has proved far more stratified than capitalist ones. We have not become equal even in poverty; and fraternity is impossible in a concentration camp. The bureaucracy has used Marx's formula to turn the state into its own private property. *It* has no desire to live in poverty.

It is our country, not the West, that in the twentieth century has experienced decay and dehumanization in every aspect of life. In the meantime, the Western nations have learned from our negative experience and have advanced along the road of socialization. In post-industrial society, unpredicted by either Marx or Lenin, private property in its classic form has been replaced by various forms of collective property, including joint-stock holdings. And the legal and proprietary guarantees of democratic institutions have given society sufficient clout to control its leaders, keeping in check the bureaucratic itch for power.

When a worker buys shares, he changes his status of hired laborer for that of co-owner. It is Western democrats who have created arrangements such as this and defused class confrontation. What are we to do? We can return to the crossroads where our histories parted company and Russia plunged into the abyss of communist utopia. In other words, we ought to return to the fold of European civilization, and to this end reinstate private property, especially privately owned land.

Of course, there is no need to revert to the robber baron capitalism of a hundred years ago. The post-industrial experience of the more developed nations suggests that powerful controls are needed to create parity between the interests of the individual and those of society. Private property is part of a larger picture. Meanwhile, not only have we tried to substitute a part for the whole, we have declared the part to be *larger* than the whole: the Communist Party has outlawed all but state property.

A joke made the rounds back when Romanov was first secretary of the Leningrad regional party committee. In an empty butcher's shop, a man curses the name of Romanov. He is rushed to the KGB. A KGB official politely asks him in what way Comrade Romanov has displeased him.

"The Romanovs ruled Russia for three hundred years but didn't stock up enough food to last for seventy!"

He had a point. We wanted to ride into a communist future on the gravy train of past accomplishment. We kept squandering the nation's human, social, natural, and moral resources. All the "successes" of the communist doctrine, from the victory in the war against Germany to space flights, from ballet to literature, were borrowed from the Russian Empire. We were gnawing away at our past. Could we hope for a future?

Social progress is set in motion by individual freedom and initiative. This is not to say that private property is a guarantee of social prosperity. The fascist regimes in Germany and Italy in the '30s, like Chile's in the '70s, exploited the proprietary instinct, but were none the more attractive or civilized for it. But whereas the regimes of Hitler and Mussolini ended in military disaster, Pinochet's dwindled into political oblivion. Post-industrial society cannot exist without individual freedom.

Communist ideology seems to be explained best by a parable about a man to whom God says: "You can ask anything of me. But bear in mind that your neighbor will get twice as much." The man pleads tearfully: "My Lord, please let me lose one eye."

At long last, on the evening of December 3, 1990, a special congress of Russia's people's deputies returned the Russian farmers their right—not to own land—but to be called "farmers." Left behind were the apparatchiks' threats and admonitions and warnings that "the people are not ready." Russia's leading Marxist-Leninist, Ivan Polozkov, made a remark on that occasion that is bound to go into the history books: "Land must not be sold because it comes from God! . . ."

On the three percent of the land that is privately owned, our farmers have been producing sixty percent of the country's potatoes, thirty percent of the vegetables, twenty-seven percent of the milk, and thirty percent of the meat. Imagine what that epoch-making day, December 3, will mean to the peoples of Russia. Considering the decades of wholesale dispossession of the farmer, it is equally impressive to note that Moscow sociologists estimate that 60 percent of the nation support private ownership of land.

What the Russian Parliament voted for is not the disbanding of state-owned or collective farms, but the creation of an economy with different patterns of ownership. When I listened to the evening news program that day, I must say I envied my colleagues in the Russian Parliament who had done what we, the deputies of the Union Parliament, had not been able to do.

We must keep in mind, however, that any law will remain just a theoretical projection if we fail to make it psychologically as well as legally binding. State property lost its sanctity long ago because citizens saw it as *nobody's* property. Even the language reflects this: a person stealing from his workplace is not called a thief, but a "liberator." You steal from another person, but you "liberate" from the state; that is, you reallocate what has been officially distributed. It is no secret that officials are out there stealing, too—and *they* distribute things unjustly. So stealing is not a sin. For dozens of years the radio, and later television, played a cheerful ditty about "everything around belongs to the collective farm, everything around belongs to me." You can't steal from yourself, can you?

Slowly and painfully, our parliament has realized that without private property no other form of property is quite real.

At the First Congress, the mere mention of a private property would provoke a furious response from a factory worker or collective farmer. Reading from papers supplied by official hacks, they would swear fealty to the ideals of the October Revolution and lash out against anyone daring to break that ideological taboo. When the committee on legislation called for a draft law on property, several of us quickly agreed that it was necessary to change property ratios between the state and citizens.

At that time, the constitution identified state property as the basis of the socialist system. All other types of property were treated as secondary and subordinate. Every schoolboy knew that in the ideal case, even collective farms and cooperative property must be transformed into state property.

Our first action in drafting a new law was to change this absurd constitutional provision. We knew we must reverse the balance. Citizens' property had been deemed limited and subordinate to state property because it accrued from work at socialist enterprises. In our draft, we said, rather, that *citizens'* property was the basis of all property in the country. Next in priority were various kinds of collective property, that is, the property of work collectives: jointly held, cooperative, and so on. And, finally, property belonging to the state.

We knew from the beginning that the amount of state property must be reduced dramatically. A mechanism of redistribution was needed. *Redistribution,* not privatization—we are speaking here of all kinds of collective property, as well as private property.

The draft was submitted for consideration by Supreme Soviet committees and commissions. Opposition from conservatives was strong, but we managed to pull it through. Our job was complicated when the government came up with its own proposals after the Supreme Soviet's first session. Needless to say, the government proposed virtually no changes in property relations. The unavoidable ideological definition was retained: *socialist* state property, *socialist* cooperative and collective-farm property. . . "Socialism" was repeated as an incantation, an "oath of allegiance" to the old, Stalinist economic framework. If passed, the government's proposal would have made it totally impossible to attack the all-powerful "agricultural gulags," to use Yuri Chernichenko's term.

We won, but it seemed only experts and the bureaucrats took

note. By overturning the property pyramid, we had declared that the state must serve society, not vice versa.

Legal limitations on citizens' property were another problem. According to the law a person could own only one residence (this applied more to the rural population, because most people in the cities live in state-owned apartments. No one could own more than a specified maximum number of, for example, cattle.

Another difficulty was creating a mechanism to protect owner's rights. The law recognizes one's right to own a residence, but offers no legal recourse. Any state organization, more often than not, the executive committee of a local council can simply decide to take your home away "for state and social needs." A good friend of mine, a professor of law in Riga, has had to build three houses for himself since World War II. Each time the executive committee came along, assessed the house at minimum value, took away the land, and re-placed a dwelling built with the owner's hands and at his own expense with a garage or a highway. No one ever asked the owner's views, and he received only token compensation. In the West such compensa-tion covers both actual losses and "mental anguish." I recently heard from this poor fellow again. It seems he's had to build house No. 4. His property was again "needed by the state."

With their property interests thus undefended, Soviet people, understandably, put little stock in property. In the words of the poet, "It's a good thing to have nothing in Russia." The system knew that economically free individuals want political freedom as well.

Our draft, omitted any mention of limitations on personal prop-erty and stated that a citizen has the right to go to court to defend his interests. Now my friend in Riga can argue against his present home being taken away. Nor will it be so simple to make a resident of a city apartment move to the suburbs (usually by declaring the apartment unfit for occupancy). Historically, it is not unusual for a person to be forced out of his home, the place where he was born, where he had lived his whole life. Such moves have ended friendships, if not family relations, and forced people to change jobs and adjust to new envi-ronments, all because some municipal office wanted the building for itself or had promised it to some cooperative hotel venture.

The Law on Property adopted at the Third Congress of People's Deputies of the USSR put an end to this abuse of power. It went into effect on July 1, 1990. Many of my countrymen have since become owners of their own homes. The only thing we failed to accomplish was getting the article on private ownership of the land into the law. The conservatives would not budge an inch. Nine months after the issue was fought over at the Third Congress, Yeltsin's Russian Parliament approved the right to own land. From now on the people in Russia will say: "Yeltsin has given the farmers the land. Stalin took it away and Yeltsin gave it back."

The land issue is now more important than ever, and I am certain that Gorbachev eventually will have to vote to allow a variety of ownership patterns. But by yielding to Boris Yeltsin the right to give the land back to the farmers, a promise that helped the Bolsheviks rise to power in October 1917, Mikhail Gorbachev ironically strengthened the Russian Parliament's influence and Yeltsin's popular appeal.

We live in a country where the ideological framework remains long after ideological content has vanished. A year ago it seemed to me I had found a good way to get around the rejection of private property instilled in people by seventy years of communist propaganda. I suggested that the law refer to "a citizen's property" instead of "private property," with the thought that the absence of any legal restriction on private property in effect legitimizes it. (By the way, the Napoleonic Code does not mention "private property," either; but refers to "citizens' " property and "individual" property.) The formula, "a citizen's property," was duly written into the statutes.

But our social mentality is such that while the conservatives settled for "a citizen's property," they rebelled against private ownership of land. Agrarian deputies were in the forefront of the attack on private property. Why? Because the majority were the heads of collective or state farms, all-powerful bosses of the "agricultural gulags." Many were honest people and good managers, but in 1989, they still could not imagine that their unlimited power was coming to an end. It was not surprising that Yegor Ligachev, the most consistent conservative member of the Politburo, was placed in charge of agriculture. He retreated into agriculture for obvious reasons: the collective and state farm system guaranteed him maximum social conservatism, and consequently, support. Farmers were more dependent on their managers than a city resident on a factory manager. To leave a collective farm meant losing one's job and one's home—the only alternative being a workers' hostel in town. No wonder Russian villages were being deserted by their young people, and that hundreds of thousands of rural communities had disappeared from the map. What will the farm bosses do, now that the farmers have an attractive alternative?

At the Third Congress of People's Deputies, agrarian deputies and apparatchiks tried to scare the rest of the Congress, saying that private property would enable black market tycoons to buy up land. Without their farms, collective or state-owned, the farmers would become serfs to new masters from the "shadow economy." Unfortunately, Gorbachev himself repeated these arguments in utter sincerity. Heated debate flared up in the committee on legislation: what if the speculators were to buy up land? Finally, we came up with a formula that seemed reasonable, if a bit half-hearted—not private property, but possession of land for life without the right to sell it.

Land could be inherited or leased out for a period. A tract of farmland that was not worked for several years would be forfeited. Land provided for building or farming needs could not be taken away. If you want to sell your house, sell it, and the quality of the land and your work input would be added to the property value. The draft statute containing these provisions was adopted at the Third Congress and thereafter became a national law.

I should note that only a year or so ago, no more than twenty percent favored private property. Today, with the notion of private property supported by at least three times that number, we would have proposed a more radical law. Land sale is not the problem; China's experience shows that if a farmer does not consider the land he works to belong to him, he milks it dry and in a few years goes to town with the money he's earned. Civilized countries have legislative mechanisms to prevent land speculation.

A Great Provincial Power

For decades, we were fenced off from the rest of Europe by our own "Great Wall." It is because of this that we have become *a great provincial power* of the twentieth century. It is time for us to recognize that glasnost and the opening of our society over the past few years have opened our eyes about the world, and about ourselves. Our mindset cannot remain that of provincials. *It is time to write new laws.*

Until private property is introduced into urban life, we will have to step carefully on the streets of our beautiful cities to avoid treading in some putrid puddle or excrement. "Nobody's" houses will continue to be covered in graffiti within a week of people moving in, and the heating fail at the first hint of frost. "Nobody's" children by failed marriages will go to "nobody's" schools short of teachers, aids, and computers, and in the cafeterias, "nobody's" bread will be littered all over (and under) the tables. Shall I go on? There's no need; who among my countrymen could not finish this page? Whatever we talk about, industry or literature, book shortages or brutality in the army, our problems—material, moral, even spiritual—boil down to the lack of a sense of being one's own master. The root is the absence of property. The proletarian who, as the Marxist phrase so aptly captures, has nothing to lose but his chains, resembles a serf, or a black slave on an American plantation. The same is true of a collective farmer or Soviet theater director, a factory worker or engineer. Without respect for property, there is no social protection, and no self-respect. And a person who does not respect himself can only despise, or at best envy, his neighbor.

The pitiful plots given to farmers for household needs and to urban dwellers for gardens have yielded incontestable proof that both rural and city people can work, and work extremely well. The Sinyavinsky Bogs, which were clogged with matériel during the seize of Leningrad, later were given over to urban gardeners who have now made them the most productive land in the Leningrad region.

As we legalize private property, we must, of course, pass laws to prevent society from sliding toward "primitive" capitalism. We must take care to protect the elderly and needy, the children and the disabled, and to save the land from speculation. We must save our society from the "nomenklatura capital" being so painstakingly legalized through all manner of "joint ventures" created with the money of the disintegrating party.

There is no point to copying blindly what cannot work here. Learning from the rest of Europe does not mean borrowing what belongs to the West alone.

The percentage of private property in the West's multifaceted economies always will be greater than in Russia. Collective ownership of both the means of production and land has long been our national tradition. When the collective and state farms built by Stalin are disbanded, many farmers will decide against individual farming in favor of cooperative or collective farming, but on a shareholding basis, with the right to claim their share of the collective product.

Similarly, major factories in Leningrad certainly will not pass into private hands. They will become joint-stock undertakings involving, in addition to workers and engineers, banks and local government bodies. The latter must also become shareholders if the interests of society and the workers are to be balanced. We will have to learn how to create popular enterprises capable of competing with one another, with private interests, and with the West. I believe that popular, joint-stock and cooperative undertakings will suit Russia best. Indeed, the Russian people's flair for collectivism was ably exploited by the Bolsheviks in 1917.

The peoples of Russia will never become English or German. Just as Orthodoxy differs from Catholicism or Protestantism, a nation's soul can never be satisfied by merely borrowing from foreign life. The best the West has to offer will take root in domestic soil, while anything in conflict with it will die away.

Since Peter the Great, Russia has been groping in vain for its own identity. First, we borrowed German bureaucracy and philosophy; then, French Voltairianism; later, Marxism. In borrowing, we violated our own culture and nature and this, too, say our Russian philosophers, is a national hallmark. But it seems to me that our national distinctiveness lies primarily in Russian idealism and collectivism. These two staunch pillars of Russian life, reinforced by imperial totalitarianism and a readiness to sacrifice life for an idea, determined our path in the twentieth century.

I am neither a Westernizer nor a Slavophile. I am just a Russian who understands that my country no longer has a right to social "experiments." We must learn from the Japanese, who borrowed Western technology, but not the Western way of life. As the second millennium draws to a close, we should also decide which Western technology we can put to good use, and which we can do without. It would be absurd to create another consumer society on the threshold of environmental disaster.

In Vyra, a village near Leningrad that was extolled by Pushkin and Nabokov, there lives a restoration architect, Alexander Semochkin, who has expounded his fascinating (if controversial) ideas on both Leningrad and Moscow television. I was particularly taken with his notion of vitalizing the twenty-first century economy by developing an economic system consistent with the laws of a living organism. The urban economy should be deindustrialized. Semochkin suggests that waste-free factories must be built at a distance from towns, while the city itself becomes the focal point of science, arts, and skilled crafts. Industry should produce semi-finished products. Detailing would be done by hand. Apart from machines and vehicles, the objects that people live with must be humanized; hand-crafted items will always be more fit and lasting companions of human life than the machinemade. And, more importantly, they will bear the inimitable imprint of artistry, the hallmark of things made in the pre-industrial age. Rural life, while taking advantage of the comforts of civilization, would be free to return to rustic simplicity in which the land is worked with care instead of with chemicals and mechanical power. The horse will be restored as the symbol of the Russian village, for although the tractor is best for plowing, it is really a crime to drive one into the woods to pick up a felled tree.

To turn back to the issue, economists often call our collective farms "pseudo-cooperatives" because a farmer who wants to quit is not permitted to take his share of what he produced. The essence of the cooperative arrangement is shareholding. This includes not only material and labor input, but also risk and responsibility. Stalin eliminated the shareholding principle in 1931, and since then, a farmer has only been able to escape from a collective farm as he would from jail or exile. Originally, the collective property of farmers and collective farms became the property of the party bureaucracy. Although a new law governing cooperatives was adopted in 1987, it does not say a word about shareholding.

Crazy? Yes, it is, but crazy in a new way. Whereas the absence of a shareholding provision in the 1931 collective farm statute reflects the fact that collective property was being placed under state control, the latest pseudo-cooperative provision conceals a kind of entrepreneurial, private ownership. Without shareholding, the organizer of a cooperative, on his own or together with his companions placed in key jobs, becomes the effective owner. The other workers are only hired labor without any say. Their sole interest is to be compensated for their labor. It is, in effect, a capitalist undertaking concealed under a "socialist" cooperative cover. A worker without a share can be fired. Without a share, he cannot monitor the activities of the pseudo-cooperative's bosses. And he has no interest in the quality of his work, the modernizing of production, or investment in new technology.

The striking thing is that the shareholding principle *was* written into the original draft of the property law. But, failing to show elementary common sense, the Supreme Soviet and government de-

leted it as "alien in a class sense" to our society. They tended to see
shareholding as the basis of individualism, and incompatible with
Soviet principles. It is a good thing that the law did not prohibit
cooperatives with property shares, and that some clever individuals
saw this as a possible basis for initiative. Many non-share cooperatives, however, failed as a result of crippling taxes imposed on all
cooperatives and the fact that these pseudo-cooperatives were
doomed to lose out in competition with state-owned enterprises. For
a cooperative to be able to maximize its potential, every employee
must truly feel he is his own master, because he has a share in the
business. By supporting each other and taking initiative as equal
partners, small-sized cooperative undertakings can compete with
state-owned enterprises whose hired labor has less interest in work
and is less efficient. Regrettably such competition remains only a
theoretical notion.

Orthodox Marxists choose to forget that even Marx called hard-
earned private property "socialist" in nature. More important, strictly
speaking, neither Stalin, nor Lenin, nor Trotsky can be called Marxists. Karl Marx believed that socialism could be built only when the
capitalist organization of production based on commodity production
had exhausted itself. Only after the further development of commodity production has become impossible can socialism take its place.
Marx predicted the triumph of socialism simultaneously in all countries precisely for this reason.

By 1917, capitalism had not yet exploited even one-hundredth of
its creative potential, and what Lenin did by proclaiming a transition
to socialist revolution in Russia alone was to provoke not the birth of
a new society, but a miscarriage—the undemocratic Bolshevik regime. Even worse, as the old Assyrian saying has it, *inside this still-
born baby there was another*: the communist regime in Russia
contributed to the growth of fascism in Europe. Fascism appeared
and rose to power in Germany and Italy as terrified capitalism's response to the October takeover. Both Lenin's international and Hitler's national radical socialism were phenomena that Karl Marx had
warned against. Marx, a great scholar, was the last of the German
Fausts, for whose services Mephistopheles exacted a grisly price. A
teacher is responsible for his pupils, and for their inability to oppose
those pseudo-disciples who "creatively develop" the teacher's most
erroneous concepts.

In post-industrial society, commodity production has not yet
exhausted its capabilities. It is true, however, that beginning with

Franklin Roosevelt's reforms, capitalist economy has become increasingly socialized. But I do not think advocates of the theory of convergence are absolutely correct. Socialism as a socioeconomic system has not yet been seen—not in the so-called socialist countries, at any rate. What we have is a kind of totalitarianism concealed beneath "scientific" communist phraseology. Convergence means the drawing together of capitalism and socialism; but what is there to be drawn together? How can a post-industrial democratic society, shot through as it may be with vestiges of old-fashioned capitalism, be reconciled with the undemocratic regimes imposed by communist bureaucracy?

Only evolution through reform gives society a chance to survive. Bloody revolution is part of a cycle of violence that peaks in counterrevolution. Marx predicted correctly the future socialization of capitalism, although he failed to realize that a transition to a humane society through the bloodletting of revolution and dictatorship was *a priori* impossible. (Dostoyevsky, a contemporary and opponent of Marx, was the first to say this.)

Western society has imposed stringent limitations on rights of property owners, making their interests subservient to the interests of society. This is socialism pure and simple, socialism as an idea and an ideal, not the political regime or bureaucratic declarations of communists.

In the summer of 1990 I was invited to the United States to lecture at Saint Petersburg University in Florida. I stayed for a few days at the president's house, which stands on the shore of a bay with a tangled forest behind it. I was surprised to hear it belonged to him. The neighboring properties, although much smaller, were better tended, with tennis courts and lawns.

"Why don't you clean up the weeds?" I asked.

"I'm not allowed."

He had no right to fell a single tree on his land without permission from the authorities, granted only on grounds of absolute necessity. His deed of purchase allows renovating only after a design is approved and a permit granted by municipal authorities.

His ownership rights are limited by community interests, including environmental considerations. Local officials say the loss of just a few trees would be detrimental to Saint Petersburg's environment.

According to the writer Tatyana Tolstaya, an American friend of hers is reluctant to have her own city apartment remodeled, because the laws of the state where she lives stipulate that, as part of any renovation, the entrance must be changed to ensure easy wheelchair access. None of her friends or acquaintances is handicapped, but the city is adamant.

I am not saying that America is perfect. Americans are terribly attached to their luxuries. Still, it is American society, not ours, that is imposing restrictions on itself. For instance, smoking in public places is widely prohibited. Efforts to save the human environment are being made on a much larger scale as well. There is no doubt that in the coming decades commodity production and exchange will also be changed and perhaps limited, for environmental disaster has become a greater threat than military disaster. Only a society in which all citizens, rich and needy, strong and weak, are guaranteed a life of wellbeing, deserves to be called humane. But there is no way we can build such a society in only one country, or even half the countries of the world. Because the earth's environment is indivisible.

The socialist idea of security, stability, and confidence in the future has been attained—by our partners, not by us. But we too will attain it. Supporters of "pure" socialism are doomed to extinction in the third millennium. Marxism, like every abstract doctrinaire scheme, has been condemned by history.

The Communist Party's increasingly obvious moral degeneration makes a mockery of the idea of communism as an alternative avenue of human development. It is clear that the people around the world share a destiny. Humanity's division into "camps" collapsed along with the Berlin Wall and under the ruins of modern totalitarian regimes. The going certainly will be tough for us. But the going is even tougher in China, where economic reforms have outrun political evolution and the surviving party structures succeeded in reasserting their grip in power through the bloodshed and massacre of the summer of 1989.

I am no prophet, but I have no doubt that before long, China will return to the path of democracy.

The twentieth century, a century of world wars and revolutions, communism and fascism, and of weapons that could destroy our planet many times over, arrived a bit late in 1917. And it expired a bit prematurely—in 1989 in Eastern Europe, and now in my country. True, any break between the economy and politics is fraught with the threat of military dictatorship. But ever since the Russian Parliament gave the land to the farmers, the nomenklatura has been doomed, even if it stages a military coup. Bayonets cannot prop it up for too long. People eat with spoons, not guns.

Only a fraction of the nation remains captive to communist illusions. The destiny of communism in Russia is decided: it has expired in people's eyes.

11

The System Syndrome

The Victims of the System Will Still Be with Us

O n my way to work today, I was struck that I was so naive to think that I would actually get to see theater and museums in Moscow. Even thoughts of such leisure activities recede into irrelevance. Seeing people who visit me in my hotel room in the mornings and, after sessions, in the evenings, people at their last tether, not knowing how to help them get their wrongs righted, I have had to learn to preserve a certain emotional distance, or every day would become a moral torment.

Many of my callers are ill or hapless victims of Soviet reality. I am beginning to see some specific, Soviet "kinks" that can only be products of socialism. I may not be qualified to offer a medical diagnosis but I feel justified in calling the symptoms I see an illness—the "System Syndrome."

A person injured by the system sets out to seek the truth and makes the rounds, not expecting much. He merely wants to uncover the truth and redress the injustice. Another letter or visit to an official will wrap things up, he hopes. With the injustice righted and misunderstanding resolved, he'll be able to return to his old way of life. It's all so simple . . .

But the system drives him into a corner, and the further he's driven, the more brutal it becomes. He amasses piles of documents bearing the most authoritative signatures, official responses typed on stern-looking letterheads. These pieces of paper give him hope as they waft him on to the next level of authority. What follows is expectation, then despair, and, in the end, often true illness.

It is a maze of mirrors refracting a glimmer of human fate, driving hope into infinite realms of paperwork, an unreal world of bureaucratic abstraction, socialist in form and inhumane in substance. There is no way out of the maze of instructions, form letters, and faceless officials.

A former person turns into a suppliant humanoid, his life sapped by the system.

Two cases remain etched in my memory.

The first was a talented former head designer from Chelyabinsk. Despite an excellent track record, he had been dismissed unjustly from his job seven years earlier. He had been offered other jobs, but refused them demanding complete justice; that is, to get his old job back. I phoned the appropriate minister and he promised to reinstate the designer in a similar position and give him an apartment.

"No, I want *my* job back," the man protested.

Unfortunately, the job no longer existed. The organization from which he had been fired in the early 1980s had been shut down.

It is an insane system, a crazed maze where weak souls get lost and trapped inside.

Pushkin captured this mentality in his "Bronze Horseman." I must retell this "St. Petersburg Tale" for the sake of the foreign reader. A terrible flood starts on November 7, 1824, in the capital of the Russian Empire. A poor clerk is stranded on top of a marble lion behind a statue of the tsar who founded the city "below the sea." Evgeni craves to get to the Vasilievsky Ostrov where his sweetheart and her elderly mother are waiting for him in the Galerny Harbor near the bay. Finally, the water subsides and he takes a boat to the other bank of the Neva river. He runs like mad, past overturned wood cabins along his way, to the house of his loved one. And this is how Pushkin conveys the moment he goes insane:

> *Here was the suburb now. With bated*
> *Breath he did stop to look. Revealed*
> *To sight, the bay stretched grey and lonely.*
> *Her house, he knew, stood near it . . . Only*
> *Where was it? Where? . . .*
> *   He moved away,*
> *Then stumbled back in stark dismay.*
> *This was the spot, a willow growing*

Nearby . . . Had house and fence been borne
Away by floods? . . . He walked with slowing
Steps all around . . . Wild words were torn
From him in spasms, by fits of laughter . . .

Pushkin's message is incisively clear: Evgeni can see that the gate is gone, washed away, but he cannot believe the house is gone. The same applies to the designer from Chelyabinsk. To get back to where there is no going back to, and to find what is not to be found—this is the "System Syndrome."

The other person I recall was a woman who had been fired from her job in a grocery store for failing to account for two crates of strawberries. She had left her husband and children.

"How are you making out in Moscow?"

"Trying to beat the odds."

"But you must live on something."

"There are good people everywhere. I'm doing odd jobs."

"Let me help you get a job in a store. We'll see justice done together."

"No, I must prove I can do it on my own."

You cannot help these people. They will never break out of the vicious circle or abandon their "System Syndrome," nor will it ever let go of them. I myself was in danger of falling into this trap when I defended my graduate thesis on cost-accounting in Soviet industry. In it I supported what is now called the market economy. I argued in favor of leasing, work collectives, and liquidating failing enterprises. The thesis got through the Scientific Council (by eighteen votes to three, with one abstention), though I had to fight for it. The presentation lasted from 3 P.M. until midnight. But when my thesis was taken to Moscow, incredible things began to happen. The manuscript got lost several times. When it was found, the attached documents had disappeared. I was being sent off on an endless trek. I would have to spend years restoring my papers and documents and go to Moscow hat in hand. Then I got word from a colleague of mine: if I patched things up with the influential people who disliked me and repented, there would be a fair chance that I would win formal approval for my thesis.

"Thank you," I said, "I'd rather write another." Which I did several years later.

It is very important to stop at the right moment when you are defending your interests, but it is different when somebody else's interests are involved. Our people distinguish between "truth lovers" and "truth seekers." A person searching for the truth for himself is usually considered a "truth seeker." After he has been injured, relentlessly, he gropes for support in high places. The outcome is a foregone conclusion. Officialdom instinctively shuns "truth seekers," even the likes of Andrei Sakharov. This attitude has become so deeply ingrained that we tend to see any opponent as a political intriguer or careerist. Sad to say, the tide of political activity has brought to the surface more than enough of such people.

One generation after another of our people has been forced to deny the instinct of defending one's nearest and dearest. Our society has been left sorely in need of mature political institutions, opposition parties, free labor unions, legal guarantees, and fair legislation.

Little wonder, after Pushkin's Evgeni confronted the monument to the tsar with the words "Just wait!" the bronze horseman chased him through the city all night. If we are to believe Pushkin, the madman did find his happiness: he found his sweetheart's house on an island in the Neva where it had been carried by the flood. But he only had enough strength to get to the porch of the ruined hut. Evidently, he did not even enter the house. He did not seem to have realized his loved one was dead and her house empty.

Society must find a way to stop before reaching the abyss, even if it is on the brink.

Theater director Mark Zakharov, with his usual wit, told me:

> I walk into the theater. The carpenters are putting together the set for my new production. I feel they've done something wrong. I don't know what it is, but I know it's wrong. I try to get involved but they say they'll cope without me. I feel badly and leave. I walk past a construction site. And again I see something . . . And then I say to myself: STOP. Because when you start seeing only what's wrong, take a pill and go to bed.

True; we build, and heal, and teach, as if in a funhouse mirror. And it is no use trying to correct the situation by fiddling around, because you will just lose your own skill and go crazy. Every People's Deputy has to deal with several visitors like mine every day. Others go to newspaper offices, procurator's offices, courts, ministers or party committees.

In the summer of 1990, dozens of people afflicted by the "System Syndrome" pitched tents in front of the *Rossiya Hotel* in Moscow. In Leningrad, after any electoral victory by the democrats, there will be someone out there fasting beneath the statue of Nicholas I on horseback. It's easy to diagnose the "System Syndrome." What you have to do is talk to a person and find out what he or she is after. These people seldom demand justice for others. They only want justice for themselves. And the main criterion is their motivation: whether it is lack of hope of being able to do one's work and live one's life, or a maniacal urge to ford the same river twice. The irony is that Russia's true heroes never asked for anything for themselves; such selflessness is a national tradition.

But when communism took root in our soil, it reduced human life to a farce, rendering a great people absurd. The imminent prospect of the system's collapse proves that the instinct for self-preservation has survived in our people. A few decades more of our "through-the-looking-glass" existence and the people would be doomed. Many traditions and social customs have already been lost. A bit longer and this process would become irreversible.

At two or three in the morning you hear a knock at your door. Though the hotel is guarded, victims of the "System Syndrome" steal their way in, tacking their missives to the door or tying them to the doorknob or pushing them under the door. The first day after I was elected chairman of the Leningrad city council, I had to receive dozens of visitors. Certainly, not all of them were yet sick, but almost every one was truly infected. It would have been a sin not to help them before it was too late.

In the first days of my Kremlin service, I was at a loss as to how to proceed. I had to prepare for each session, go over documents, look for weak spots in the legislative proposals. But I also had to help the people coming to see me.

It did not take me much time to collect the "autographs" of virtually every top state official. There were some vague replies dismissing (with or without good reason) my requests to assist someone. But I also received some good news: "Housing has been provided . . . ," "a job has been given following your request . . . ," assistance has been given . . ."

I must admit that my requests addressed to the military have proved the most productive of all. And their replies have been the most concise and to the point. The Defense Minister and his deputies respond to deputies' requests in good time and often with good results. But this, too, is the consequence of the system; it can operate only within a militarized framework (as Stalin, its creator, was well aware).

And One More Episode

Walking in an almost empty underpass from the Supreme Soviet Presidium to the Kremlin, I hear a woman's hysterical voice calling to me: "Anatoli Alexandrovich! . . ." I stop. There's a crazed look in her eyes: "Do you remember me? You appealed on my behalf a month ago. My boy was sentenced unlawfully to ten years and imprisoned for four. Look, this is a Supreme Court ruling. He's free." She seems ready to fall on her knees, I give her a hand up and realize that her eyes are glittering with joy. She has come to Moscow just to share her happiness at having her son, and her own life, back.

A mother never pleads for herself. So long as there is a glimmer of hope, so long as her boy is alive, or she *hopes* he is, going crazy is a luxury she can not afford.

It can be the same with wives. Maria Rozanova (the wife of writer and former political prisoner Andrei Sinyavsky) appearing on the TV program "The Fifth Wheel," said she had gone to the KGB to try to have his seven-year jail sentence reduced. She told them, You and I want the same thing, for Sinyavsky to get out of prison as soon as possible. I don't need to explain why *I* want this. And you want it, too, because you didn't quite realize whom you were dealing with. So long as Sinyavsky remains behind bars, the West will curse you every single day, and you'll rue the day you imprisoned him. And besides, he's written a book in the camp and passed it on to me. If he serves out his full sentence, or if anything happens to him, he'll owe you nothing, and the manuscript, which is now in a safe in Paris, will be published.

Maria Rozanova got her husband out of jail more than a year before the end of his term. She had not told the KGB that the "camp book" was just the essay "Walks with Pushkin," a manuscript Sinyavsky had sent to his wife quite legally in the form of letters.

So the bottom line is this: don't ask for anything for yourself. This rule must be observed, because the total "collectivism" of our social organization ensures that it is every man for himself. The system is utterly indifferent to the individual's fate.

But the more a deputy is showered with complaints and requests, the more he comes to the sad conclusion that this is not why he was elected to Parliament. Our social disease can be cured only by saving the individual from the terrible oppression of the system and placing him on a par with the state.

What else is on the mind of a People's Deputy as he goes to work in the Kremlin?

The law must be the same for all. It must be as unchanging as the standard measure of length or weight. Anything else is an offense against the law and an abuse of civil rights. Even before Bolshevism was imposed, there was a Russian saying: "The law is like a steering pole." As the state went on steering it willfully, and the people went on a crime spree, they matched state crime with personal lawlessness. Circumventing the law became habit; there was no other way to survive. Let's admit it: hardly any of us hasn't broken the law at least once. To get crime under control, we must first establish the rule of law. Unfortunately, the authorities keep providing precedents for licensed abuse. However one feels about the "controversial" KGB general Oleg Kalugin, stripping him of his decorations and pension benefits was legally reprehensible.

Authority's intentions are not always malign. Part of the problem is that human relationships have been uprooted, moral rules and principles have crumbled, and the habit of anarchic behavior has become so strong that removing it will take years.

"You Were Kind"

I am increasingly convinced that abnormality is the norm for an ordinary professional politician. As I watch the everyday life of state officials, I am scared of getting entangled and becoming a "pro."

An intellectual normally keeps up to date with literature, reads periodicals, goes to the theater, and listens to music. He chooses new friends after his own heart, keeps his family and old friendships intact, and longs for fresh emotional, intellectual, and spiritual impressions. Professional politicians miss out on much of this. True, they may go through the motions of enjoying the arts—top national leaders visit the Bolshoi once a year, the Moscow Art Theater once a decade. But they never see what the whole town is talking about. Films are less of a problem; they are screened at the dacha.

I am not being sarcastic. Daily overwork teaches a politician to ignore "trivia." One's personal and intellectual development are stunted. The ratified environment in which our politicians exist, oblivious to what worries people, is their reality. The posh dachas, villas, and mansions, the special foodstuffs checked for radioactivity, the home movies, all the luxuries of nomenklatura existence—these are small compensation for the beauty of the human world they have foresworn. In return, they get a warped through-the-looking-glass view of state deceit, and sincere bewilderment about the simplest everyday things.

The blame is not entirely with the system. Even in civilized societies, a professional politician is doomed to squander the intellectual, moral, and spiritual capital he has accumulated in earlier years. I find it easier to work in the Supreme Soviet than do many of my colleagues. For one thing, a politician must be a lawyer of sorts. I held on to my capital longer than most. But I am already beginning to feel that I am wasting my potential without making up for an iota of what I have given away.

My daughter says I was a different person before. How so? *"You were kind."*

Children can see right to the core. Sadly, I must admit that a politician lives in a no-man's-land isolated from normal human relations. Politics brings out the worst in people. When one is unable to cleanse one's soul, one is tempted to make up for what has been lost at the expense of others and by newspaper and television exposure. And the sweeter the solace feels to you, the more you have lost.

You cannot be a politician all your life. Politics is like a trip to outer space. But a spaceman cannot be confined to his orbiting station forever. Likewise, a professional politician must someday "return to earth." In the past there were men who rose to the top of the political pyramid and volunteered to come down with the intent of rejoining politics after enjoying a period of grace in which they could absorb new knowledge and ideas and analyze their own mistakes and failures.

Politics is rightly called the art of compromise. Practicing this art changes one's values, but this deformation is invisible and unremitting. When we watch a politician on television saying something incongruous and exclaim: "But he doesn't understand anything," the last thing we are ready to believe is that he really *doesn't* understand. He has used up his stock of humanity and knowledge; he is living on a drug called politics.

The process whereby a human being "slides" into officialdom has not yet been studied by our social psychologists or by writers. It seems, however, that with non-professional politicians coming to the fore in Eastern Europe and here, science and art soon should have a great deal to say about this phenomenon. Under totalitarian conditions a talented working-class youth became a helpless functionary whose only role was to embody the state's proletarian essence. Today, the people who fought the system are coming to power. But they cannot always tell when democracy ends and egoism begins.

Opposition to totalitarianism must confront the danger of new totalitarian structures replacing the old, as happened in Russia in October 1917. Remember the Bolsheviks campaigned under democratic slogans and even traced their descent to the Russian Social Democrats.

I have profound respect for Lech Walesa and Vaclav Havel. I am sure of their integrity and commitment to democratic principles. But, as non-professional politicians, these democrats must take special care not to adopt the "professional methods" of the old regime.

We understand this—in words. But as for our deeds . . .

We are all infected to some degree by the system. From birth, we have been taught intolerance, suspicion, and paranoid fear of spies. Even our democrats tend towards political monopoly. Not to mention orthodox Marxists and pro-fascist groups like Pamyat . . . It makes the current economic crisis particularly perilous: only when our nation can feed itself will we be able to say that democracy has *triumphed*.

If we overcome the system's resistance and build a market economy, powerful democratic forces capable of preventing any relapse into the past will appear. Then we, the pioneering deputies, will feel free to go back to our private lives. We are mere recruits, and most of us dream of completing the work that was suspended in spring 1989 until better times. I dream of my books, my research, and the joys of life within a Russian intellectual's compass.

I am fond of authors of antiquity, but when I read Tacitus, Plutarch, or Cicero before, their words about the difference between the life of a private individual and the life of a statesman were mere abstractions to me. Was the gap so great? But now I know whereof they spoke.

The risk of getting bogged down in the self-regulated system of official routine is too great to be shrugged away. Stereotypes of officialdom are too contagious. The pressure on a new leader is unrelenting.

But these are fears for the future. In the meantime, as I go to

work in the Kremlin, I think about the frayed tempers of yesterday's rally and the intransigence of people who see themselves as democrats but trample on others' rights. And there is another peril—the physical violence that threatens us all. If the government and the president fail to act in time, society's passions may sweep away the fragile democratic structure superimposed on the as-yet-unchanged mechanism of totalitarianism. Few of us will survive if discontent comes to a head and sets off a chain reaction of unrest. In such chaos, leaders' good intentions will be worthless.

My more cautious and experienced colleagues see my behavior as mad; they spread their arms in wonder when they meet me and say: "You at least could think of your family!"

They do not know I have already had the threatening phone calls, the attempts at setting me up for blackmail. My country's future is on the line, however, and it is too late to try and sit it out. Our history confirms that you can't ride out the storm in the quiet of your study or laboratory. So many of Stalin's victims kept a low profile and never opposed the advent of totalitarian rule. The more active people stood a better chance of surviving, by emigrating or by making the most of the protection, fragile though it may have been, of their professional affiliations. One could hide under one's bed and still lose everything to a neighbor's whim to turn one in.

As I walk to the Kremlin, I know that the nation will remain at the crossroads for another couple of years. I must stay with it all the way, not give up until the system has been buried—as the great man who charted the system's course in October 1917 and who still lies in state must also be buried. The city where I live was named by its founder after Saint Peter and was later renamed in honor of that unburied man, Lenin, whose cause has yielded such terrible fruit in every corner of the globe; Lenin, who did indeed realize that things were going wrong, but could do nothing to correct them.

The confrontation between the left and the right will continue for a few years. The fragile political equilibrium, the economic crisis, and the attempt to break with the totalitarian past—painful, for blood is being spilled—will go on for some time. But as soon as we realize that in a normal, civilized state there is enough room for both radicals and conservatives and that there is no need to slaughter half the population to make the other half happy, we will be treading on the firm ground of legality and social justice. Meanwhile both the authorities and democratic organizations must shy away from the specter of new bloodshed.

Only in the last two years have I fully realized the value of private life and personal freedom. It is worth living for the human right to a private life, even at times, worth fighting for. Politics is an unavoidable, albeit distasteful, element of modern society; to a great extent, it shapes your life, whether or not you are directly involved in it. Still, it is a surrogate life in which the true seeds of human individuality are sublimated. In politics, individuality fades away.

All politicians, even the most progressive, are guided by impersonal considerations. When everyday you see people who have been schooled in government (and especially Soviet government!), you recognize that they have been cut to a standard measure, and you realize they are prepared to obey every instruction from above or adapt to any regime. They serve the state machine—an inhuman task, inhuman as any zealotry or passion for revenge. What you must suffer for is not an idea, or yourself, but your fellow man. Then your life will have meaning. A priest prays to God for other people.

As I walk along, I dream of the day when I can quit politics with a clean conscience. I appreciate what the poet David Samoilov calls "the popular imagination at work," that is, myths and legends about rulers giving up their power of their own accord. I do not find at all fantastic the apocryphal tale of Tsar Alexander I giving up his crown to retreat to a remote monastery or to travel across Russia. As a young man, Tsar Alexander was a liberal. He attempted reforms, contemplated freeing the serfs, and granted Poland its constitution. But there is a limit to any person's ability to oppose the machinery of state. All the more so if he is a weak personality, and in private life remains an autocrat, a statesman who is not free even if he wields virtually unlimited power. I like the legend about the tsar's escape because it is full of faith in humanity and a yearning for a full life.

The last Russian emperor evinced a touching desire for a private life, even though it went against the interests of state. True, Nicholas II was not the butcher professional revolutionaries made him out to be—he loved and was loved, and simply longed to be happy with his own family. Still, Alexander Solzhenitsyn rightly blames the government for what happened to Russia in 1905 and 1917, because it did not save the country from Bolshevism. The Russian emperor was an honest man in the wrong job. The January 9, 1905 shooting of peaceful demonstrators headed for the Winter Palace to plead with the tsar for justice is an object lesson for today's democrats: the totalitarian system has no mercy on either its subjects or its leader. Entrust the future of the nation to the secret police and the military, and you become a political puppet. The executions of January 9 are on your conscience because you embody power, even though its immediate cause is a struggle of interests and ambitions between the clans and cliques of the top echelon.

Indeed, it is a lesson for any democrat who acts indecisively as leader of a city, a republic, or the whole country. The system can provoke him cunningly into making a decision that, while seemingly innocent, even civic-minded, can produce catastrophic results. If the system provokes bloodshed behind the back of a reform-minded democrat, he will not be able to wash away the blood and claim innocence.

An intellectual who decides to enter political life should refresh his conscience and historical memory. Like an ancient navigator, he runs the risk of confronting the twin evils of Scylla and Charybdis: degeneration or physical violence. We, the deputies of the first democratic phase, have faced both these monsters. Perhaps future parliaments will be free of these temptations, and so will be able to work better and more sensibly to build a democratic, law-governed state. But their peaceful efforts will have been paid for by our tribulations.

On the map of Moscow, the Kremlin looks like an irregular triangle. Here, as in the Bermuda Triangle, time goes at a different rate. The triangle is also the geometric figure which best describes what goes on in Parliament. At two corners, the left and the right, we have radical democrats and neo-Stalinists. Between them lies the rest of the spectrum: democrats, liberals, centrists, and conservatives of all shades. The apex symbolizes supreme authority, today embodied by the president of the USSR.

Like the Kremlin triangle on the map of Moscow, the parliamentary triangle is irregular. Its apex shifts to the left or right as authority responds to the dynamics of the forces below. The center of gravity is never still.

Mikhail Gorbachev is understandably fond of talking about consolidation. In the early phases of perestroika, he used a metaphor about a boat that needed to be kept steady. Later the word "consensus" appeared in our political parlance. If supreme power responds flexibly to the changing social balance, it will be possible to achieve consensus despite criticism from the two corners. In fact, our social boat must rock if it is to go forward.

But if it takes on water, it is not the crew who is to blame, but the captain and his officers. They have chosen the wrong tack, or ignored the weather forecast or the economic reefs ahead. So the appeals not to rock the boat are not very sensible. A good captain can do without coaxing, for he has both a pilot and a helmsman—his programs and his government.

Still, the metaphor is fairly accurate, at least when the captain's hands are tied and the rudder is stuck. This was the case in the second and third year of perestroika, in the nascent phase of Soviet parliamentarianism, and before Article 6 of the Constitution was deleted.

Our social boat is headed for a democratic law-governed state, a multiparty system, and a market economy. If we don't get rid of the dangerous ballast—the crippled party structures, the political organs in the army, the repressive agencies, and the awesome burden of the command economy with its ministries, state property, and all the structures we have inherited from the utopian dogma of Marx and Lenin, from the bloodthirsty ideology of class elitism, and from the years of Stalin's rule and stagnation, and we don't get rid of them fast, we will capsize and sink.

Without drastically revamping the existing power structures, we won't be able to make any headway now, just as we could not without repealing Article 6 of the Constitution some time ago.

I am sure that as a politician Mikhail Gorbachev must be aware of this. It is another matter that as president of the USSR, Gorbachev must have his own reasons: the apple falls when it is ripe. Not before. In any case, it is not the job of a president to shake the tree.

To get back to the parliamentary triangle, the weakening of power is a situation in which the "left" and the "right" are so distanced from each other that the vertical line of power is no longer vertical. If the left or right corner, or both, shift away from the center, and if political polarization assumes threatening dimensions, the apex must rise just as quickly. Then the vertical line of power will be restored and harmony restored for some time.

Instituting the presidency during spring 1990s critical days of social ferment enabled Gorbachev to save the vertical line of power from collapse, and spared the nation a massive upheaval. The presidency enabled the national parliament to survive until local and republican governments were elected.

The Congress of People's Deputies of the RSFSR, the election of Russia's Supreme Soviet with Boris Yeltsin as its chairman, and the democratic city councils of Moscow and Leningrad—all were instrumental in propping up burgeoning democracy and staving off explosion from below or a rightist putsch.

But our long–suffering economy still struggles with the constraints of the old system, and the punitive organs and the army have
not been democratized. The economic crisis is escalating. Society
rapidly is becoming polarized. These conditions promoted the president to request extraordinary powers, which were granted by the
USSR Supreme Soviet in late September 1990. With the vertical line
of power thus hitting the ceiling, only dictatorial power lies above:
emperor's crown or a generalissimo's epaulets. At that height there is
no need for parliament, or constitution, or elected government. The
parliamentary triangle cannot be stretched any further; it will just fall
apart. The least damaging option would be to insert a new vertical
line of power by replacing the bankrupt leader with one more popular
and flexible. The worst that could happen would be for parliamentarianism to collapse, an autocratic or totalitarian state take its place—
the triangle shrinking to a bloody point, a new dictatorship.

The president is the chief executive. But Anatoli Lukyanov,
answering written questions at the Third Congress of People Deputies, interpreted the presidential powers more broadly: "The President at the supreme level coordinates and brings together both
legislative power—the power of representative bodies, and executive
power."

Clearly, in this case, parliament might turn into a mere advisory
body to the head of state, and the president would become an autocratic ruler who would disband the "unnecessary" parliament just as
Nicholas II disposed of the State Duma.

Well, I promised to avoid politics, but it keeps creeping into the
story.

Our Last Citizen-Prophet

It seem I was not alone in having politics intruding uninvited into my
life. Millions of Soviet people went through this in 1989. Andrei
Sakharov had gone through it twenty years earlier.

Sakharov was not a politician, but politics probably killed him. I
am thinking of the arduous and futile preparations for a general warning strike which never took place. It is a bruising experience to pour
oneself into an effort that comes to naught. Only the young and
healthy can stand it.

Sakharov acquired a large following only after his death—a fate more often seen among prophets than political leaders. He was our last citizen-prophet. There is no one to match him now, nor will there ever be.

Victory for the prophet comes through death, not battle. And all of Russia, the entire nation, walked behind his bier.

But we listened to him without hearing him. The First Congress of People's Deputies did not support his draft Decree on Power (realistically, it could not have done so under the political conditions then prevailing). We will be paying the price of this failure for years to come.

What else as I head to the Kremlin?

Boris Gidaspov told a reporter that as a boy he was a *lapta* (the Russian variety of baseball) player, and a great fighter. I cannot claim such past glory. I never fought with my hands or feet; at most, I would move in with my elbows. Hence my frequent falls from the top.

As a boy, living in Kokand, where we moved from Chita, I wanted to be a teacher. A math professor's family evacuated from besieged Leningrad lived next door, and my mother did her best to help them out, supplying them with goat's milk. I was impressed by the spirit of intelligence and education in that professor's home. I wanted to be like him and began to dream naively of becoming a professor.

The best thing in the world, though, was food. I had friends and kind parents, there were lots of dogs in the streets—but not much food. I still remember that feeling of hunger which would never let go of me. Our goat was the only reliable source of food. My parents could not afford a cow, nor was there enough grass to feed one. A goat was easier to keep. Mother used to give my brother and me baskets to pick grass. One day someone hit the goat with a stick, and it became ill and died. I have never since wept as I did then.

Our parents never punished us. Once I stole a cigarette from father's cigarette-case. I just wanted to try one. He had a long talk with me. I don't remember what he said, but I never smoked again.

I became an avid reader, again thanks to the professor from Leningrad. My favorite characters were D'Artagnan, Huck Finn, and Tom Sawyer. I read what the curriculum required about Lenin. I do not read books about Lenin to my daughter. When she was in kindergarten, her teacher said she should read a story about Lenin with her parents. In one episode, Lenin walked through a park and saw a farmer felling a tree. He stopped and said: "I forgive you this time, but if it happens again . . ." Ksyusha, who had heard a lot of law talk since infancy, asked me: "Daddy, Lenin was a lawyer like you, wasn't he?" "Yes, he was." "How can a lawyer order someone around without a court decision?"

Then, when she heard the Supreme Soviet was to be rotated after a year, she picked up the new word right away:

"Daddy, are you going to be rotated soon?"

I have reached the end of my walk. I go through the Kutafya Tower, say hello to the polite Kremlin guards, and continue on a short and gentle ascent to that crystal pillbox, the Palace of Congresses.

We will be forgotten some day. I am not a religious man, but I hope to God that people pray for us now.

Epilogue

After the Bloody Sunday in Vilnius

In December 1990–January 1991 the political and economic situation in the country reached a crisis. Instead of the anticipated stabilization, we have witnessed a sharp turn to the right. People have begun to lose all hope in a better future.

What happened?

First it was Eduard Shevardnadze who, by his resignation, clearly and courageously warned the country and the world about the looming threat of a dictatorship. Then in the Baltic republics we witnessed attempts at a coup d'état with the aid of the military. These atttempts failed in the face of the people's staunch resistance and determination to defend their right to independence whatever the cost. They were followed by decisions which had an adverse effect on the economic situation, intensified inflation, and put thousands of industrial enterprises on the brink of stoppage and closure.

In March 1990, when the Congress of People's Deputies of the USSR elected the first President of the Union of Soviet Socialist Republics, the democratic deputies were guided by the realization that the division of functions between the party and the state should be effected as quickly as possible.

We believed that Mikhail Gorbachev would base his actions on the interests of the people. His decision to retain the post of General Secretary was only the historical demand of a particular period of time.

The events of the next few months showed that we were right in assuming that the election of Ligachev or one of his ilk as general secretary would have posed a danger. The harsh criticism of the President by radical conservatives at the Constituent Congress of the Russian Communist Party and at the 28th CPSU Congress was proof in point.

Why did the same people who applauded Ligachev and heckled Gorbachev pension off the former and re-elect the latter as head of the party?

Party leaders who formed the core at the two forums realized that by voting Gorbachev down they would only strengthen the processes of perestroika. They would only doom themselves to an early political death, since the President would then rely not on the Communist Party but on the democratic forces of the country, and the Communist Party would be forced out of the political arena. When Boris Yeltsin, Gavril Popov, and I told the 28th Congress that it was impossible for us to be simultaneously leaders of Soviets and members of *any* party, the democrats continued to put their faith in the President's common sense.

The constructive dialogue and agreement made by Yeltsin and Gorbachev in August 1990, the latter's support of the Shatalin-Yavlinsky program of economic reform which offered a real chance of overcoming the crisis, the President's unequivocal recognition of the necessity to pass from vague slogans about socialist orientation to the market economy, and the rejection of the government's pathetic program for making this transition, prompted a feeling of optimism. Decisive economic steps seemed imminent. The President could not fail to see that the gap between political and economic reforms was becoming truly dangerous.

However, at the most crucial moment of choice, when everything depended on the President and, I genuinely believe that the civic courage of a single individual could have saved the "500 days" program at the Supreme Soviet, no such courage was displayed.

It is difficult to say now why this happened. It is no secret that the will of the country's leader was broken by the merciless force of the nomenklatura. The plan for economic reform was replaced by an absurd set of so-called guidelines. This utterly vapid and senseless document was a "guideline to nowhere" which led Nikolai Ryzhkov's government into a blind alley.

The President, whose strength had been sapped by that decisive moment, could not maintain his position. The first to realize the nature of that retreat—more like a flight from the battlefield—were the President's closest adherents and aides, in fact, the best and most loyal of them.

Although we often use the words "the President's team," Gorbachev never had a team of his own. He had had to fight party functionaries for most of his political career during the perestroika period. It was a dramatic struggle, during which he came to an uneasy understanding with some people while getting rid of others. From time to time whole groups of opponents of the new course were tossed overboard. Gorbachev negotiated reefs skillfully, always in the minority and showing miraculous ingenuity. But when he began to be surrounded by intelligent, strong, independent, and highly competent people who enjoyed the respect of the whole country, he failed to perceive the qualitative change among his closest associates. Accustomed to working among the time-servers of the party pyramid, he overlooked the experience and wisdom of his aides and supporters.

Yakovlev, Shevardnadze, Bakatin, and Petrakov were the first to take note of Gorbachev's rejection of the cause he himself had initiated. One after another, they left him.

As a reformer risen from the party apparat Mikhail Gorbachev could not give due credit to the devotion of those people, to the principles and ideas which were until a certain historical moment the essence of the democratic reforms; in fact, his own essence. And, unfortunately, he allowed the reactionaries to organize the scurrilous baiting of his allies, the defamation of Alexander Yakovlev at the Third Congress of People's Deputies of the USSR, and the campaign against Eduard Shevardnadze on the eve of the Fourth Congress. When a general berates the Minister of Foreign Affairs (a Politburo member) in brusque and abusive "commander's" terms and the head of state and the party pretends to "hear no evil," the head of state is in trouble, as I believe the President was aware.

It was a turning point in Mikhail Gorbachev's political life.

Then came a tragic error, Gorbachev's attempts to hold the country together with the help of military force in the Baltics. History has long since passed its sentence on such political practices. Ligachev, giving a radio interview during an interval in a plenary session of the Central Committee sometime last year, said that the country's leadership had grown wiser since the days of Czechoslovakia and Afghanistan and now realized that political questions could not be decided with the help of tanks.

Gravest of all was the President's refusal (not for the first time!) to admit his participation in such "political dialogues." After the bloody night in Vilnius and the storming of the building housing Lithuanian television by paratroopers and KGB personnel, the President stated that he knew nothing about the events.

This statement, together with similar pronouncements by the Defense Minister and Minister of the Interior, and the televised speech of the KGB Chairman, who also tried to justify the shooting of peaceful civilians, produced a distressing impression all over the world. When a country's president hastens to shift onto the rank-and-file responsibility for actions of which he cannot be unaware, and which had had such tragic consequences, he violates his presidential oath.

This alienated Gorbachev not only from democrats, but also from the military who were sent to pacify the independent Baltic republics only to learn the next morning that they had "acted on their own cognizance."

Loss of confidence is a fatal blow to a political leader. True, a dictator may lose the trust of the people but retain power if he enjoys the trust of his associates, or of the bayonets defending his throne or presidential chair. But no one can remain active as a politician if he loves both the state power structures and the generals.

And this is precisely what happened.

The President failed to become a real president of his people and remained general secretary of the CPSU Central Committee, the very party which lost the faith and support of the people. The party failed to offer the country a way out of economic and political impasse, a fact our people will never forget.

April 1989, Tbilisi. January 1990, Baku. January 1991, Vilnius.

A commission of the Congress of People's Deputies of the USSR has established that Gorbachev was not involved in the massacre that took place in front of Government House in Tbilisi. But he did nothing to bring to justice those guilty of the events of that terrible night. The film shot by KGB cameramen has not yet been shown on television. But the situation has been changing since April 1989 when the General Secretary was an object of the reactionaries' plot. Troops in Baku lay idle while Armenians were subjected to pogroms, and tanks stormed Azerbaijan's capital, also at night, only after the pogroms ceased and after the First Secretary of the Central Committee of Azerbaijan's Communist Party fled the city and power virtually passed into the hands of the Popular Front. The action was sanctioned by a decree of the Chairman of the Supreme Soviet of the USSR, and those who implemented it did their best to make the bloodshed as copious as possible. A year later, the President appeared to be closer to the forces of the past era.

When he became a hostage of the reactionaries he ceased to be a democrat and a reformer. Thus, the General Secretary conquered the President.

Tbilisi, Baku and the Baltic republics. These three landmarks have become Mikhail Gorbachev's personal drama and have determined the fate of perestroika which he launched so brilliantly in the mid-80s.

January 25, 1991

Afterword

The Failed Coup and a New Beginning

A s far as I was concerned, this book was done. I had nothing left to add. I had said everything I had to say about the events of the past two years. Every thought, every reflection was there on the page, to the last detail. Finished, I heaved a sigh of relief. It had been a long and difficult task. But life had another idea. "Life," in this case, being the attempted coup d'état of August 19–21, 1991. And so, I was forced to go back and add this afterword.

Over the past year, there has been a great deal of talk in both the domestic and foreign press about the threat of a military coup, and much discussion of the possibility of a dictatorship. Doubts were raised about just how secure the process of perestroika was, and whether the drive to democracy in our country was truly irreversible. Thinking back, it seems to me that there was a lack of faith in the future based on our unsteady control of the changes we had put in place, combined with the haunting knowledge that time was running out. We knew all too well that the political and military establishments were not about to cede their power without a last-ditch fight. And that's exactly what we got.

In contrast to the many others who have described the coup less as a case of democracy triumphant than of a junta self-destructing, I want to stress that it might easily have been a successful coup, with far-reaching implications, *had the people remained silent.*

Now that the coup has failed, people have been puzzling over its "inexplicable" lapses. For instance, why weren't Yeltsin, Sobchak, Popov, and other democratic leaders arrested? Why didn't the coup leaders use the military force at their disposal rather than just parading it menacingly? In reality, matters were less mysterious—and more sinister—than they may have appeared on the surface. First of all, the coup leaders could not adopt such seemingly "routine" measures, for a coup, as arresting the democratic leaders after isolating the President because Yeltsin, Popov, and I were not just a handful of democratic activists, but popularly elected representatives of what has become a government of law. Before arresting or otherwise imposing restrictive or repressive measures on duly elected representatives, the Gang of Eight had to be sure they would not find themselves confronting an angry citizenry in the streets. The conspirators decided it was safe to isolate Gorbachev because they were convinced that his popularity had reached such a low level that, once he was out of sight, the people would accept his removal from office without a murmur.

But the coup leaders hadn't a clue what the public was thinking. They were just a band of opportunists, without any popular backing. Take Pavlov, with his financial reforms abruptly removing various denominations of currency from circulation; or Kryuchkov, with his universal schemes of denunciation and spying on citizens; or Yanayev, an absolute nobody, whose inveterate womanizing and drinking were so well known. They could not count on any popular support, and this was a central factor limiting the action.

But most important of all was the general public's reaction to the coup. The inhabitants of Moscow, Petersburg, Sverdlovsk, and other major cities poured out into the streets by the thousands to demonstrate in defense, not of their personal property, but—for the first time in Russian history—in defense of the *rule of law.*

Two key facts were evident in the coup's failure. First, the communist system, in its many decades of existence, had produced a uniquely undistinguished breed of functionaries. Talented, bright, independent-minded individuals were destroyed, and all power was allotted to faceless mediocrities. Tomorrow, no one will remember these "faceless people," each man for himself and himself alone, representing no one, and—this was crucial—unwilling to take responsibility. Not one of them had the nerve to be accountable for the bloodshed and deaths that might have resulted if force had been used against the people.

I know for a fact that the conspirators tried to get Yazov to take personal responsibility for signing an order to storm the White House—Russian Federation headquarters—and Marinsky Square. And there were other attempts by members of the junta to get Pavlov and Yanayev to take over official leadership of the plot. But, knowing that they had absolutely no popular support, cut off from the people, and seeing only negative reactions to their initial move, they did not dare take this step, thus dooming the coup. Still, it must be said: even such an utterly "faceless" coup might well have succeeded *if the people had remained silent.* Khrushchev's ouster in 1964 was also the work of "faceless" nonentities; Brezhnev, Suslov, and the other members of the group that removed him were untalented, unoriginal mediocrities. But then, the people remained silent. Today, millions of people found in themselves the will to resist. What we witnessed was truly the birth of a free nation—a freed people founding a nation built on freedom. We watched what can only be called the birth of a civil society. This is what the coup taught us, and it is the great hope for our future. This lesson was clearest, of course, to those most determined to avoid any return to communism.

But there was another aspect to this coup that should not go overlooked—the wait-and-see attitude, the hesitation, on the part of military and KGB personnel that prevented the junta from putting the military machinery into action that first night. Now that the coup has been crushed and democracy has arisen triumphant, I want to make a special point of praising—not those who never wavered, who had long since chosen their path straight to the barricades—but those who hesitated. For it is precisely those thousands and thousands of waverers—the militia and KGB personnel, soldiers and officers—who sent the coup to its downfall. We must appreciate those who doubted the ability of might to defeat the people, and help them seize the belief that no other life is possible for them and for their country than one based on the struggle for freedom and democracy in the name of our children and grandchildren and of their future.

To really appreciate what took place during the coup and its lessons for the future we must reconstruct the events themselves. What happened on the morning of Monday, August 19, was unexpected for all of us. Certainly, I can attest to the fact that it came as a shock to Yeltsin, Popov, and myself. If a coup was in the offing, people thought, nobody expected it to happen the way it actually did. The Extraordinary Session of the Supreme Soviet of the USSR, which we had just concluded, had actually given us some uneasy optimism. Even though it was non-commital in its decisions, it managed to

instill hope with prospects of aid, investments, and increased economic cooperation.

I spent Saturday and Sunday, August 17 and 18, in Lithuania. I
was there for discussions with leaders on a direct economic exchange
agreement between Lithuania and Leningrad. We had concluded the
agreement, and I had also met with representatives of a number of
political groups and parties. Satisfied at having finished a good week-
end's work, I flew off to Moscow on the evening of August 18.

The next morning, I was scheduled to get down to work as a
member of the delegation making preparations for the signing of the
Union Treaty. That evening, I paid a visit to Alexander Yakovlev. We
talked about prospects for our democratic reform movement, and
Yakovlev showed me a letter he had written to the communist party
in reaction to recent events, including his own expulsion from the
party. I got back late from his place and went straight to bed. Since
I had not had much sleep for the past few nights, I slept like a log, as
though I had fallen into a bottomless blue abyss.

I was awakened by the harsh ring of the telephone at 6:30 A.M.
A journalist friend was calling to report that there had been a coup
d'état. He had just had a call from Kazakhstan, where three hours
earlier they had received documents from a so-called "state emergency committee." As it happened, a state of emergency had been
declared countrywide, and President Gorbachev had been removed
from power.

The first thing I did was look out the window to see if the
building was surrounded. The coast was clear, meaning I would not
have to go to the neighbors to plan the next step. The building's
residents were all members of the USSR Supreme Soviet. I phoned
for my car and security personnel. The duty officer for the day was
Oleg (for obvious reasons, I will omit his surname here), but the other
guards who awaited me were from Yeltsin's entourage. Yeltsin, I
learned, expected me at his dacha in Usov, outside Arkhangel.

Tanks were trundling along, of all places, the Ring Road:* a very
bad joke. One tank, burning on the side of the road, was filling the air
with filthy smoke. Of course, no one had actually set it on fire. We've
just got such talented operators at the controls. Further on, there was
a more ominous sight: a group of paratroopers. But they let us past.

Yeltsin's dacha was guarded by a half dozen or so people with
automatic weapons, but that was all. As I walked inside my heart

---

* The main highway circling Moscow—*ed.*

stopped: the entire leadership of Russia was sitting there, and a single commando could have knocked out the whole government. Yeltsin asked for my advice. I suggested that he convene the Russian Parliament, and keep it in continuous session.

He said that they had reached the same decision, and that the text of an appeal to all the citizens of Russia would be ready any minute. Then we had to decide whether to stay here or get out. Opinion was divided. Either way was dangerous.

Khasbulatov, head of the Russian Supreme Soviet, said, "I'm taking off as soon as I have the text. You can decide for yourselves."

The text was brought in, and Khasbulatov left for the White House. (Apparently, he took a private car in hopes that he would not be recognized and stopped.)

I insisted that we had to follow Khasbulatov and just shove our way through. Was there some other road? I was worried about those paratroopers on the Ring Road. I was told there was no other way, except on foot. "Well, this *is* a presidential convoy," I said. "Let's raise the state flag and get moving. But hurry!"

As Yeltsin put on his bulletproof vest his daughter said, "Papa, take it easy, everything depends on you now." No one said a word about the fact that Yeltsin was clearly upset, not even his wife, Naina Yosifovna.

I asked Yeltsin whether I would be needed at the White House, or whether I could return to Leningrad. He said, "Go back." I told him, "I'll stick with you as far as Kutuzovsky, then we'll see if we get through." If we did, I planned to head back to the Ring Road and on to Sheremtyevo Airport.

Thank God, the paratroopers were gone. Maybe they had gone to the dacha to pick us up, and we passed them along the way, or another bunch had been sent to the dacha too late. We later found out that they had missed us by ten minutes.

We raced along behind our militia escort—cars, tanks, armored vehicles made way for us. Escort vehicles were covering Yeltsin from all sides. We whizzed by the Ring Road and onto Rublevka. It is a narrower road, but the armored vehicles yielded here too. Thankfully there were not too many of them. After making it through we were finally on our way to the airport, where we hit another snag. The next flight to Leningrad was not for two hours.

I later found out that orders for my arrest had been issued, but here again, the coup leaders dropped the ball. Instead of assigning a special group to pick me up, they relied on the airport KGB. The agents had agreed—but apparently not too enthusiastically—to arrest me. Three of them showed up and flashed their IDs as I sat in the airport's VIP lounge. "Watch out," I said to Oleg, and he answered, "I know one of them." The three disappeared into the airport bar, and Oleg followed them. They emerged all together. Two of the agents, as it turned out, were from the special unit assigned to stamp out black-marketeering of currency, and said they were planning to guard me right out to the runway. So now I had four guards, three with machine guns.

As soon as I could, I called Leningrad and ordered the OMON special military forces to guard the TV studios. I found out that General Samsonov, commander of the Leningrad Military District, had already announced over the air that he had taken over my position, but troops had not yet been sent in.

I did not know until afterwards that there had been plans to arrest me at the Leningrad airport, but the head of Leningrad's internal affairs department, Arkady Kramerev, sent out a special forces car to pick me up and whisk me to military headquarters. My guards, who waited for me downstairs, later told me that one of Gidaspov's aides who had been hanging around stuck his tongue out at them behind my back. When we got up to the second floor and the commander's office, the door was ajar, and the room empty. "What's going on here?" I yelled, "The General's office left unguarded?" A colonel hustled to the door to meet me. Normally, he wouldn't let me in, but now he saluted me: "Take me to the commander." "Yes, sir! They're in there, meeting." "Well, let's go!" I said, and we went back down to the first floor. They were all in there: Samsonov, Kurkov (KGB head), Savin (commander of the interior troops), Viktorov (head of the Northwest Border District Command), and, of course, Boris Gidaspov, the region's party chief, its head communist. Also there was Arkady Kramerev, a democrat and a good friend.

They were shocked to see me, so taking advantage of their confusion, I launched into a speech before they could get their mouths open. I admonished them by reminding them of General Shaposhnikov, who in 1962 refused to open fire on demonstrators in Novocherkassk, told them that in the eyes of the law they were conspirators, and if they lifted a finger, they would be facing a Nuremberg of their own. Then I appealed to Samsonov: "General, think back to Tbilisi; you were the only one there who acted like a human being, refused to carry out a criminal order, stayed in the shadows.

What are you doing getting mixed up with this bunch—this illegitimate gang?"

SAMSONOV: "Why 'illegitimate'? I have orders . . ."

"Look, you know I helped draft the law on emergency powers. There are only four situations which permit a state of emergency to be implemented in a specific territory. Has an epidemic broken out here?"

SAMSONOV: "We're just implementing it as a precautionary measure . . . I have an order . . . a letter . . ."

"Show it to me."

SAMSONOV: "I can't. It's classified."

"Then tell me if it contains these words: *'Institute a state of emergency in Leningrad.'* "

"Just as I expected. Remember General Rodionov at the First Congress of People's Deputies. He, too, overstepped his orders. He was ordered to secure military installations, but he ended up sending out his troops against the people. Are you asking for what he got?"

GIDASPOV: "What do you mean, yelling at us?"

"Shut up, you. Can't you see that you're destroying your own party by being here? You should be out on the streets, shouting that the CPSU isn't behind this . . ."

GIDASPOV: "The economy's in tatters, industry's fallen apart . . ."

"Nonsense. Leningrad's industries surpassed the economic plan for the first half of the year. (To Samsonov): "I ask you, please do everything in your power to keep troops from entering the city!"

SAMSONOV: "I'll do what I can . . ."

We drove to my headquarters at Marinsky Palace. Vice Mayor Vyacheslav Shcherbakov had just returned from a trip. I met with the head of the city council, Alexander Belyayev: "We have to convene a session." "It's done; the deputies have already been informed."

I headed to the TV studios just a few minutes before I was scheduled to appear on a live telecast. With me were Shcherbakov and Yarov, the regional council chief, both of whom the junta members had included on their committee without permission. We got there five minutes before airtime. The head of Leningrad TV, Boris Petrov, had even arranged a satellite hook-up, so we were seen far beyond the borders of Leningrad.

While on the air, it occurred to me to refer to the Moscow junta members as the "former" this (vice president, minister of defense, etc.) and "former" that, and then just plain "citizen," as though they were already sitting in the dock. Even though there had not been any popular resistance to the coup by that evening (the city council had not yet convened its session), the joint appearance of the mayor, vice mayor, and regional city council head would at least have broken through the thicket of paralyzing confusion.

Following the broadcast, we kept the OMON forces busy. Kramerev and Shcherbakov were running between the Marinsky Palace and the military command's headquarters. An endless stream of people kept on coming up to me with new details of the plot. One visitor really sent a shiver down my spine. Introducing himself, he showed me ID stating that he was a former general staff colonel and told me he was in on the early part of the planning for the coup, a year ago or more. He said one of the suggestions made then was to bomb the Leningrad reactor in order to create havoc and use it to take over.

Meanwhile, Samsonov was under fire from Moscow. The members of the junta were screaming hysterically over the phone that he had sold out to the democrats. At the same time, we learned that two columns of military equipment were moving towards the city from the south. Barricades were needed, but it was clear that we would not have time to build them. The tanks would be here within the hour. We found out that there was some heavy equipment around the airport, like trailers, steam rollers, and paving machines, capable of blocking a highway in a matter of minutes. As the tanks moved past Gatchina, Pushkin's ancestral home, Samsonov gave me his word as an officer that he would not allow them to enter the city. The column turned at Gatchina. For three days, the tanks would stand motionless at the military airfield there.

How did Shcherbakov and I manage to persuade Samsonov? I am not really sure, but I think common sense won in the end. We asked him, "General, can't you see what nonentities these people are? Even if they get hold of power, they will never manage to hold on to it."

The tension was dissipated a bit when we linked up with Yeltsin. Then I grabbed an hour's catnap on the sofa in my office. At 6:00 o'clock in the morning, I went to Putilovsky (now the Kirov factory) before the start of the new shift. A car with a loudspeaker was parked and waiting in front of the factory. We held a small rally, after which the manager's office distributed passes to the workers so anyone who wanted to could attend the rally we were calling for the whole city. As I left, a column of three or four thousand people was already turning onto Stachet Boulevard. I wanted to lead the people to the rally in Palace Square, but my security guards advised me not to.

At 10 A.M., the whole city was in Palace Square. We had to divert entire columns of people onto distant approaches. The square is wide, but nothing so wide as this ocean of people. We had decided to ask everyone to return to their workplaces by 6 P.M., and that's what happened. No one skipped work. I was told later that even the convicts in the prisons asked to be allowed out onto the barricades, promising to return afterwards to their cells.

Among the speakers was the distinguished elderly historian, academician, patriot—and now, folk hero: Dmitri Sergeyevich Likhachev.

It was clear that the coup would not make it in Leningrad.

Towards evening, I came up with the ideal plan: to get Yeltsin to name Shcherbakov military head of the Leningrad region, including the city, maybe even personal representative of the Russian president and the Russian Committee of Defense as well.

But what were Yeltsin's people thinking? A fax arrived, appointing Shcherbakov head of the Leningrad Military District—this was a potential disaster. Samsonov would be at my throat. And such an appointment would not even solve the tactical problems; we had a naval base and a border command to worry about, too. Just as I expected, Samsonov phoned: "What's going on behind my back?" I assured him that it was just a mistake, we were fixing it up. But the radio broadcast the announcement before we could stop it. I explained over and over on the phone to Moscow what we needed. Finally, we got what we needed from them.

At 3 A.M. there was more news: the military command's special forces—the commandos used to seize hijacked planes from terrorists—had just been deployed from Kalyaeyev Street to the mayor's office.

Said Shcherbakov, "Our whole militia plus all of OMON is no match for these guys; they can polish us off in five minutes." We agreed to split up. I headed to the Kirov factory, called the director, and explained the situation. But thank goodness, we did not have to rouse the Putilov plant workers from their beds.

I had been trying to reach Anatoly Lukyanov for two days on special high frequency phone lines. I kept on hearing that he was not in, he was busy. Finally, on the morning of August 21, I reached him. By then, it was clear that the coup had fallen through. Lukyanov picked up the receiver himself and started to talk about how he had been looking all over for me, how he wanted to do something "really radical" and get on a plane and fly to the Crimea. "Let's see if they can keep me, the chairman of the Supreme Soviet, from seeing Gorbachev," he said. I endorsed the idea. Whatever we could do to get back in touch with Gorbachev more quickly was worth doing. I told Lukyanov to get going and do whatever he could to free Gorbachev.

The defeat of the coup d'état, and the victory of democracy, have brought us a greater hope for the future—but we are also left with a residue of despair and distrust. Americans like to use the expression, a "self-made man." The sum of our system of protectionism, nepotism, and graft has been the disappearance of any equivalent expression in the Russian language. Faced with a successful individual, all we can think to ask is: "Who backed him? Whose protégé is he?" The legacy of the communist system is a looking-glass world in which the original and talented are persecuted and mediocrity rises to the top.

Added to this is our economic crisis. According to our Constitution of 1977, our national patrimony—our wealth—belongs entirely to the state. No one owns anything. You can work your whole life long, and never acquire one stick of property. It is urgent that we make our people property owners and teach them to respect the property of others, in order to reinstate the dignity of the individual, and thereby the dignity of our society and of our nation.

These are great and historical tasks whose resolution will take years, if not decades. Today, however, we have a chance to make a leap into the future, and swiftly realize an economic and political transformation.

But putting first things first, we must take extreme care not to harass or alienate the thousands upon thousands of functionaries who have suddenly found themselves without jobs. We must not hound them into exile or drive them underground. On the contrary, we must do everything possible to give them faith in the future, and a new perspective. We must afford them the opportunity to do work that serves their society. Under no circumstances should we give in to the temptation to engage in denunciations, "witchhunts," the sort of activities that were so characteristic of the purges that took millions of victims and warped our lives for decades.

That all may seem safely in the past, but the dead can so easily "put their claws" into the living. Today, the future of our country depends solely on us. It is contingent on the extent that we, the people's elected representatives, people with governmental respon-

sibilities, the professionals, the entire intelligentsia, manage to discard the past and move into the future unafraid of new ideas, to break with the old stereotypes and patterns which have ruled our lives for decades. The fate of communism in Russia has been resolved, once and for all.

Humanity has been fortunate enough to escape yet another dead-end ideology, another theoretical scheme dreamed up by nineteenth-century thinkers convinced that they had a recipe for salvation from suffering—a recipe that came very close to being fatal, not only for our own people, but for all of humanity.

This gives us the strength to regard the future with hope. It gives us reason to believe that Russia and the other peoples of the former Soviet Union may return to a united, civilized family of nations. Then, it will be possible to live a life worthy of humanity.

August 1991

Index